e
2.6.08

A Practical Guide to Teaching Science in the Secondary School

A Practical Guide to Teaching Science in the Secondary School is a workbook designed to support student teachers, trainees and newly qualified teachers learning how to teach science. With a strong practical focus, which deals directly with teaching in the school science laboratory, it will help teachers build on their basic skills and increase their broader knowledge and understanding.

It contains all the advice, guidance and resources that new and student science teachers need to reflect on and develop their teaching practice, helping them to plan lessons across the subject in a variety of teaching situations. Helpful features include:

- case studies
- examples of pupils' work
- examples of existing good practice
- a range of tried-and-tested teaching strategies
- activities in each chapter to help student science teachers analyse their learning and performance
- web links for further reading on evidence-based practice.

Designed to be used independently or as an integrated extension of the popular textbook *Learning to Teach Science in the Secondary School*, which provides detailed examples of theory in practice, this book is packed with examples of how to analyse practice to ensure learning is maximised in the classroom. Students, trainees and newly qualified teachers will find this book an invaluable resource because of its concise, direct style and comprehensive coverage of all aspects of science teaching.

Douglas P. Newton was a teacher for twenty-four years before he began training teachers. He is currently a Professorial Fellow at Durham University, UK.

Routledge Teaching Guides
Series Editors: Susan Capel and Marilyn Leask

These Practical Guides have been designed as companions to **Learning to Teach [Subject] in the Secondary School**. For information on the Routledge Teaching Guides series please visit our website at www.routledge.com/education.

Other titles in the series:

A Practical Guide to Teaching Physical Education in the Secondary School
Edited by Susan Capel, Peter Breckon and Jean O'Neill.

A Practical Guide to Teaching History in the Secondary School
Edited by Martin Hunt

A Practical Guide to Teaching Modern Foreign Languages in the Secondary School
Edited by Norbert Pachler and Ana Redondo

A Practical Guide to Teaching Citizenship in the Secondary School
Edited by Liam Gearon

A Practical Guide to Teaching ICT in the Secondary School
Edited by Steve Kennewell, Andrew Connell, Anthony Edwards, Cathy Wickens and Michael Hammond

A Practical Guide to Teaching Design and Technology in the Secondary School
Edited by Gwyneth Owen-Jackson

A Practical Guide to Teaching Science in the Secondary School

Douglas P. Newton

 Routledge
Taylor & Francis Group

LONDON AND NEW YORK

First published 2008
by Routledge
2 Park Square, Milton Park, Abingdon, Oxon OX14 4RN

Simultaneously published in the USA and Canada
by Routledge
270 Madison Ave, New York, NY 10016

Routledge is an imprint of the Taylor & Francis Group, an informa business

Typeset in Palatino and Frutiger by
Keystroke, 28 High Street, Tettenhall, Wolverhampton
Printed and bound in Great Britain by
Antony Rowe Ltd, Chippenham, Wiltshire

British Library Cataloguing in Publication Data
A catalogue record for this book is available from the British Library

Library of Congress Cataloging in Publication Data
A catalog record has been requested for this book

ISBN10: 0–415–45364–X (pbk)
ISBN10: 0–203–93205–6 (ebk)

ISBN13: 978–0–415–45364–6 (pbk)
ISBN13: 978–0–203–93205–6 (ebk)

Contents

List of figures, tables and tasks

FIGURES

TABLES

TASKS

Abbreviations

ASE	Association for Science Education
BECTA	British Educational Communications and Technology Agency
CASE	Cognitive Acceleration in Science Education
CLEAPSS	Consortium of Local Education Authorities for the Provision of Science Services
CPD	Continuing professional development
CPSHE	Citizenship, personal, social, moral, spiritual, cultural and health education
DART	Directed Activity Related to Text
DfES	Department for Education and Skills
ESD	Education for Sustainable Development
GCSE	General Certificate for Secondary Education
ICT	Information Communications Technology
Ofsted	Office for Standards in Education
QCA	Qualifications and Curriculum Authority
SAT	Standard Assessment Test

Series editors' introduction

This practical and accessible workbook is part of a series of textbooks for student teachers. It complements and extends the popular textbook entitled *Learning to Teach in the Secondary School: A companion to school experience*, now in its fourth edition, as well as the subject specific book, *Learning to Teach Science in the Secondary School: A companion to school experience*. We anticipate that you will want to use this book in conjunction with these other books.

Teaching is rapidly becoming a more research and evidence informed profession. Research and professional evidence about good practice underpin both the *Learning to Teach in the Secondary School* series and this practical book on teaching science. Both the text and subject specific books in the *Learning to Teach in the Secondary School* series provide theoretical, research and professional evidence-based advice and guidance to support you as you focus on developing aspects of your teaching, or on your pupils' learning, as you progress through your initial teacher education course and beyond. Although the text and subject-specific books include some case studies and tasks to help you consider the issues, the practical application of material is not their major focus. That is the role of this book.

This book aims to reinforce your understanding of aspects of your teaching and support you in aspects of your development as a teacher and your teaching. It should enable you to analyse your success as a teacher in maximising pupils' learning by focusing on practical applications. The practical activities in this book can be used in a number of ways. Some activities are designed to be undertaken by you individually, others as a joint task in pairs and yet others as group work working with, for example, other student teachers or a school- or university-based tutor. Your tutor may use the activities with a group of student teachers. The book has been designed so that you can write directly in it.

In England, new ways of working for teachers are being developed through an initiative remodelling the school workforce. This may mean that you have a range of colleagues to support your classroom. They also provide an additional resource on which you can draw. In any case, you will, of course, need to draw on additional resources to support your development. Other resources are available on a range of websites, including that for *Learning to Teach in the Secondary School: A companion to school experience*, 4th edition (www.routledge. com/textbooks/0415363926), which lists key websites for Scotland, Wales, Northern Ireland and England. For example, key websites relevant to teachers in England include the Teacher Training Resource Bank at www.ttrb.ac.uk. Others include: www.teachernet.gov.uk, which is part of the DfES schools web initiative, www.becta.org.uk, which has ICT resources, and www.qca.org.uk, which is the Qualifications and Curriculum Authority website.

We do hope that this practical workbook is useful in supporting your development as a science teacher. We welcome feedback that can be incorporated into future editions. We would like to thank Tony Turner for his contribution to this book.

Susan Capel
Marilyn Leask

Introduction

This book is for anyone who wants to be a science teacher. Teaching science is one of the more interesting and worthwhile things you can do with your time, but you would expect me to say that so I ought to justify it. Teaching science lets you continue to play with a subject that, I assume, you already find interesting. Even graduates with a jaundiced view of their degree courses can find going back to what turned them on science in the first place refreshing. Unlike some subjects, you are not tied to a textbook, board or a screen, lesson after lesson. Instead, you have a more varied, hands-on existence. And when you get this varied and hands-on part right and your pupils grasp the point of it all, the satisfaction is enormous and makes it all worthwhile. Oh, and yes, there may be bad days but aren't all jobs like that? Your aim will be to create lessons that make such days rare. In the process, I hope you will also find that being creative with your lessons is a source of enjoyment. After all, being creative is supposed to be the very essence of a rewarding life. Teaching is also learning, but you only learn if you are thoughtful about what you do. This, and the companion volume, *Learning to Teach Science in the Secondary School: a companion to school experience* (edited by Jenny Frost and Tony Turner), are intended to help you make your teaching thoughtful and rewarding.

This is a book to think with. You could use it by yourself to help you think about your science teaching and develop your skills. On the other hand, you could also use it as a course book with the guidance of a tutor. But reading it passively will only do so much. Active engagement is what matters. For that reason, tasks have been provided throughout, so jot down your thoughts and add notes. In other words, treat the book as a consumable object and write on it. At times, you may find it useful to work with a colleague, or to work as a group, but you could do the activities by yourself if you prefer that way of working. Each chapter is organised into several short topics. You are offered one or two tasks after each topic. These tasks vary in length and nature. Some are simply checklists that help you focus on what matters. Others ask you to pull together something of practical use in teaching. Often, they let you choose from a short menu which National Curriculum topic to use as a context. To begin with, you are likely to feel more comfortable thinking about topics that centre on you own specialism so feel free to focus on these. After a little practice, try to be more adventurous, move outside your specialism and extend your skills. The tenth activity in each chapter is a problem to solve. These problems are generally to help you see the chapter in a more integrated way. You may be familiar with a problem-solving approach to learning and know that the thought and study can lead to very secure and rich learning. Altogether, this amounts to sixty activities, six of which are problems. You may attempt them all, or be selective, or be advised by your tutor. It is possible to respond to many of the tasks in a variety of acceptable ways so they have various 'right' answers. At the end of each chapter is a short list of additional sources to help you extend your knowledge of a topic, should that be needed.

Teacher training courses can be rather short. They cannot address everything you might want to know. They can, however, give you a good framework, show you how to use it and give you the tools to add to the framework as you practise. What you think and do when you work with this book could make that framework stronger and your progress faster.

Chapter 1   What underpins your teaching: matters of science and science education

Never say no to an experiment.

E. Chargraff (in Gaither and Cavazox-Gaither, 2002)

INTRODUCTION

The purpose of this chapter is to bring to your attention some matters that affect your science teaching in broad ways. How you perceive science shapes what you do in your lessons. Conceptions stem from many years of doing and learning science, so you may not be altogether conscious of them but they will, nevertheless, determine the flavour of your lessons. At the same time, your pupils will have their own conceptions of science and these will shape how they respond to your lessons. If you are aware of such conceptions you can take them into account. By the end of the chapter you should:

- know some key features of the nature of science;
- be able to justify the place of science in the curriculum;
- be aware of how you and others may think of science;
- know how models of science teaching could help you.

THE NATURE OF SCIENCE

What is science? Although you may have studied science for several years, this is not a question that crops up often, if at all. We tend to build our picture of science over time and from our experiences of it. Often, parts of the picture are fuzzy or vague so, how well do you know science? Task 1.1 is a warm-up exercise.

Task 1.1 Do you agree or disagree with the following statements about science?

Write either A (agree) or D (disagree) in the box next to each statement.

1   Science is not science without mathematics. ❑

2   Science is about precise measurement. ❑

3   Experiments can show scientific explanations to be true. ❑

4   Experiments test scientific explanations. ❑

5   The approaches to testing ideas in the various sciences are the same. ❑

6   Science does not involve opinions. ❑

7   Science establishes the truth about the world. ❑

8   Scientific explanations are tentative until proved by experiment. ❑

9   If an experiment to test an explanation is negative, that explanation must be abandoned. ❑

10 Testing explanations with planned experiments is what makes science different. ❑

11 Science is not contaminated by so-called creativity. ❑

12 Scientific laws are patterns found in nature. ❑

13 Scientific laws never change. ❑

14 Scientists invent explanations about the world. ❑

15 Being a scientist and being an historian is just the same, we both do our best to get at the truth. ❑

If you have the opportunity, compare your responses with those of a colleague then read on.

WHAT IS SCIENCE?

Science is both:

- a *process* – a way of thinking and working to make sense of the natural world; and
- a *product* – a body of knowledge produced by that process, such as explanations.

It is also an activity that involves and affects:

- *people.*

These three aspects are evident in what follows.

Scientists makes sense of what we see around us by constructing explanations of them. Given that these explanations have some face value (they are consistent with the information to hand), scientists attempt to test these explanations empirically. This often means using an explanation to make a prediction and testing the prediction in a fair way. If the prediction is shown to be wrong, the explanation is probably wrong. For example, many people once believed the Earth to be flat. They pointed to the way the surface of a long, straight canal remained in view far into the distance. Flat-earther John Hampden was so confident of this that he offered £500 to anyone who could prove him wrong. The temptation was too much for evolutionary biologist Alfred Wallace. He placed three markers at equal distances along the Old Bedford Level Canal. Each marker was exactly 13 feet 4 inches above the surface of the water. The flat-earthers predicted that the tops of all the markers would make a straight line. The experiment, however, showed, that this was not so. When the last marker was viewed from the first, the central one was above the line of sight. Was this the end of the flat-earth theory? People do not always give up pet theories easily and this one rumbled on for many years, but Wallace got his money.

When faced with a theory that has failed its test, do you immediately reject it? Scientists are human and are not always quick to reject what seems like a good idea. They tend to re-examine the experiment to see if there is something wrong with it. This is not a bad thing, up to a point, but when an overwhelming number of scientists conclude that the explanation is wrong, that usually clinches it, at least, for the majority. But what if the prediction is shown to be right? Does this mean the explanation is right? Others may replicate your test and make new predictions and test them. Eventually, a pile of positive results begins to convince others that there is something in your explanation. In the case of the round earth theory, ships disappearing below the horizon and pictures of the Earth from space make for weighty evidence (but even the latter has been discounted as a confidence trick by the last of the flat-earthers). But that is not the same as saying a theory is certainly true. At some later date, it is always open to someone with another idea to pit it against yours. In the meantime, scientists usually busy themselves exploring how your theory works, making new predictions from it, and seeing how it fits in with other ideas.

Carefully constructed fair tests are not always possible in some branches of science. An explanation of earthquakes, the expansion of the universe, or the cause of human brain tumours might be difficult to test, for different reasons. Sometimes, however, it is possible to use naturally occurring events as sources of evidence. Note also that scientists who work in different areas can have different approaches and favour different kinds of experiment. For example, the comparison of a control and an intervention is quite common in biology and in medicine but less common in physics. Even medicine has its own flavour in its liking for 'double blind' experiments. In other words, the process varies from branch to branch of science. And, in practice, scientific study and investigation is rarely as clean and tidy as this might suggest, although it tends to appear so in textbooks after the event (Hussain, 2005; Reiss, 2005). Nevertheless, underpinning all is a desire to confront ideas with sound empirical evidence. It is the seeking of empirical evidence that gives science its strength and marks it off from other ways of knowing and other areas of the curriculum. The well-founded knowledge it produces may, of course, have practical application in technology. It is through technology that the majority of people know science and they may see science and technology as one (Feynman, 1998).

Task 1.2 Why flies don't drop off ceilings

What could this case study teach a Key Stage 3 class about the nature of science?

Why don't flies drop off ceilings? How do flies hold on, even when they are upside down? People just assumed that flies' feet had suckers on them, a bit like those rubber suckers used to stick hooks on doors. John Blackwall wasn't convinced by this explanation. He knew that suckers won't work if there is no air because without air there's no air pressure to press them in place. This would

Task 1.2 *continued*

mean that flies should not be able to keep their grip inside a bottle if there was no air in it. He trapped a fly in a bottle and pumped out the air. The fly didn't fall off the bottle sides and continued to walk about as normal. What this shows is that a fly's feet can't be working like suckers. So, how do they walk on ceilings? Blackwall examined a fly's foot with a microscope and saw that it had a sticky liquid on it. He concluded that flies do not drop off ceilings because this sticky liquid holds them in place. He really needed another experiment to test this idea but he didn't do one. Can you think of one to test his explanation?

Identify what this activity could teach about the nature of science. If possible, compare your thoughts with those of colleagues. Regarding 'another experiment', what could it be?

THE IMPORTANCE OF SCIENCE EDUCATION

Science education is important because it offers:

- *a way of thinking* about the world that has application in everyday life; and
- *well-founded explanations* of the world.

A school should have a place for science because these contributions are distinctive and have had a major impact on life and thought.

It is tempting to think of scientific thinking as a single skill but it is more accurate to see it as a fairly coherent suite of thinking skills that can be brought to bear on a problem. They begin with a belief that the world can be understood rationally, they include dispositions to be open-minded, objective, even-handed, and they rely on empirical evidence; they involve creatively constructing explanations and tests of them; they embrace the need to think critically about assumptions, ideas, tests and interpretations; they include a willingness to reserve judgement when the evidence requires it. Such thinking has application in everyday life. You may, for instance, doubt the advertisement which extols the merits of a particular 'new and improved' washing liquid, or have to choose something healthy to eat, or be told that mobile phones slowly fry your brain, or are asked to vote in favour of a particular way of disposing of waste. Being able to think scientifically could help you evaluate the evidence and avoid being exploited or deceived.

Scientific knowledge, through technology, has had a lot of practical application. The lives we lead today are very different from those of a thousand or even fifty years ago. The knowledge we might gain from a science education could help us understand this technical world and live in it successfully. Sometimes, the knowledge could be of immediate practical value in that it might help us, for example, use a biological means of pest control effectively, or repair a vacuum cleaner, or avoid injury from a faulty oven. But scientific knowledge has something more to offer than practical utility. We seem to be curious about the world and need to understand it, reduce the world's chaos to meaningful structures, and feel confident in it. Scientific explanations can satisfy that curiosity and provide that understanding, meaning and confidence. The problem is what to teach. Generally, science educators tend to go for what they often call the Big Ideas in science, such as, for instance, Forces, Energy, the Particulate Nature of Matter, and Plant and Animal Cells. Is this a good choice?

Apart from what science has to offer you personally, it also contributes to prosperity through its application in industry. Novel ideas that stem from new (and old) science may generate wealth for society. Governments generally seek to encourage science education or, at least, they show concern if interest in it declines.

For these reasons, everyone should have the opportunity to acquire *scientific literacy*. Scientific literacy usually means having a grasp of the processes and products of science. The problem is that not everyone agrees with what scientific literacy means (Laugksch, 2000). Quite apart from the obvious, such as which processes and products should be emphasised, some argue that school science simply cannot give someone a scientific literacy that is up to the task (Shamos, 1995). Is it possible, for instance, to give pupils an understanding of a complex problem like global warming so that they can respond in a truly informed way? Equally, is it possible to give pupils an adequate grasp of scientific thinking so that they would be able to evaluate arguments about the possible adverse effects of mumps, measles and rubella vaccinations? By necessity, we simplify what such learners do, but does that risk making it too simple to be useful? Or, can we argue that we offer learning that is at least on the way to better things, it does not impede further learning and is often up to the task? The consensus is that there *should* be a 'science education for citizenship' with opportunities for some pupils to go further (ASE, 2006a).

Task 1.3   Scientific literacy

What do you think is essential for scientific literacy? Tick or cross each box.

1   Make pupils aware that ideas are generally tested experimentally in science. ❏

2   Make pupils aware that scientists try hard to make tests fair. ❏

3   Have pupils learn how to make fair tests. ❏

4   Have pupils develop an ability to evaluate evidence. ❏

5   Have pupils confront superstitions. ❏

6   Help pupils develop scientific knowledge to live safe lives. ❏

7   Help pupils learn science that might support a hobby. ❏

8   Help pupils understand their world. ❏

9   Have pupils learn something about the Big Ideas in science. ❏

10   Help pupils learn to apply scientific knowledge in new situations. ❏

11   Have pupils acquire and use correctly a scientific vocabulary. ❏

12   Have pupils learn some applications of science. ❏

13   Have pupils practise scientific thinking in everyday situations. ❏

14   Have pupils discuss issues such as global warming. ❏

15   Prepare pupils so they could follow a career in science or technology. ❏

If you have the opportunity, compare your responses with those of a colleague.

Task 1.3 *continued*

According to Wynn and Wiggins (1997), the five 'Biggest Ideas in Science' are:

- physics' model of the atom (a nucleus with its attendant electrons);
- chemistry's periodic table (elements grouped according to their properties);
- astronomy's Big Bang theory (explaining the expansion of the universe);
- geology's plate tectonics model (explaining the arrangement of the con-tinents);
- biology's theory of evolution (explaining plant and animal changes over time).

Focus on physics, chemistry and biology and choose a Big Idea. Could you teach it directly or would you have to prepare the way? What concepts, ideas, and background would you teach first to prepare the way? Jot them down and then put them in the order you would teach them.

SCIENCE AS OTHERS SEE IT

It is not surprising that liking, interest and achievement in science tend to go together (Singh *et al.*, 2002). Each probably leads to a little of the other. Whether or not your pupils like science and show interest depends on many things (Cleaves, 2005). For instance, mothers' views of science help to shape those of their children (Bleeker and Jacobs, 2004). This means that pupils may arrive with more or less made-up minds about science. For instance, many see science as something done by balding, bespectacled, bearded men wearing white coats, usually working alone in chemical laboratories (Newton and Newton, 1998). Even if you like a subject, find it interesting and believe it to be important, this is hardly likely to make you want to spend your life with it. As Jenkins and Nelson (2005) put it, 'Important, but not for me.' Fortunately, what you say and do in your science lessons also matters. Since being interested makes learners more attentive, engage more with the subject and want to do more, interest is something you want to foster (Newton, 2000). Unsurprisingly, pupils find some topics more interesting than others (see Task 1.4). It is easy to say we should leave boring bits out but that may not be up to you, and some topics that could be seen as boring underpin others or have value in the long term. Instead, you need to ask if they can be taught in interesting ways.

Task 1.4 Likes and dislikes

Jenkins and Nelson (2005) identified popular and unpopular topics. Study the following lists and generalise from them using the questions that follow.

Popular with boys

Explosive chemicals, how it feels to be weightless, black holes, how meteors could cause a disaster, life beyond the earth, the effects of electric shock.

Popular with girls

Why we dream and what they mean, cancer, sexually transmitted diseases, abortion, anorexia, alcohol and tobacco effects on the body.

- What type of topic is generally popular with boys?
- What type of topic is generally popular with girls?
- Is there any common ground between these? If so, what is it?

Unpopular with boys

Alternative therapies, the lives of famous scientists, organic farming, how plants grow and reproduce, plants in my area, how crude oil is converted into other materials, detergents and soaps, symmetry and patterns in leaves.

Task 1.4 *continued*

Unpopular with girls

Plants in my area, organic farming, how technology helps us handle waste, atoms and molecules, how a nuclear plant works, the lives of famous scientists, symmetry and patterns in leaves, how crude oil is converted into other materials.

- What type of topic is generally unpopular with boys?
- What type of topic is generally unpopular with girls?
- Is there any common ground between these? If so, what is it?

The study found that 'plants in my area' is unpopular with most pupils. Why should this be so? Is it something about the topic? Is it the way it is taught? Either by yourself or with colleagues draw up a list of likely reasons.

In many respects, Task 1.4 confirms the stereotypes of boys' and girls' interests. In broad terms, boys appear to be interested in control, represented here by being able to do rather extreme things with materials, while girls show an interest in appearance, nurturance and health. To what extent are these interests a product of the way that science is taught? Are there ways of presenting science that interest girls in control and boys in health? Are there different sources of interest that attract both boys and girls? Attempts are made to disseminate science and dispel inappropriate beliefs, images and stereotypes amongst adults by, for example, those who work in the area of the Public Understanding of Science but progress has been slow (Miller, 2001). In preparing the next generation, your contribution can make a difference. Remember that enthusiasm is infectious (Bettencourt *et al.*, 1983). Used in moderation (or you risk adding to the stereotype of a scientist) it can show your pupils that science matters to you and is worth their attention.

SCIENCE LEARNERS

Pupils also bring with them quite specific ideas about how the world works. This more detailed knowledge may:

- make learning easier, as when pupils believe that the world is roughly spherical (having seen pictures of the Earth taken from space that contradict a belief that the Earth is flat), or when they know that light travels in straight lines (having seen laser light shows);

- make little difference as, perhaps, when pupils know that breathing air and helium makes speech sound different;
- make learning more difficult, as when pupils believe that roots collect a plant's food, that an insect is not an animal, that it is the depth of water that makes things float, that we see by sending something from our eyes, that a force is always needed to keep something moving, that electricity bills will be high if we leave a socket switched on even though nothing is plugged in, or that balloons filled with air will rise when released.

Obviously, it is the last of these that will make you pause for thought. You may think that all you have to do is show pupils the error of their ways and all will be well. Sometimes that is true and some misconceptions (also known as alternative conceptions) are fairly easy to put right. For instance, if some pupils thinks that a 3-volt battery will give you an electrical shock, it is easy to convince them this is not true. Those who think that plants are green because they absorb green light may change their minds after lessons on the selective absorption of light by different surfaces. Similarly, those who believe that all acids are dangerously corrosive may be given pause for thought by demonstrating that fruit juices can be acidic. But some misconceptions are based on everyday meanings of terms or on years of everyday experience and seem to work well. For instance, pupils may tie together the words 'pure', 'natural' and 'good for you'. This can lead them to group chemicals in non-scientific ways and judge naturally occurring materials as being essentially safe (Lake, 2005). Many pupils believe that light things and hollow things float, a pattern of nature that, for them, is a law. They can apply their law and get it right a lot of the time. Even when you show them light and hollow things that sink, they often hold on to their alternative conceptions because they work most of the time. Bringing pupils to think in terms of relative density or displaced water and the upthrust it generates takes time and persistence. The two conceptions may exist side by side in a pupil's mind for a long time. Furthermore, it can be physically difficult to show that a conception is inadequate at times. If you demonstrate that a brick sinks in a dish, then a bucket, then a bath, then the river, then the sea, the pupil could still argue that if the sea was deeper, the brick might float. Similarly, a belief that synthetic chemicals cause diseases is difficult to contest in a practical way. And there are conceptions of how the world works that just *feel* right. For instance, it is hard to believe that it is possible to keep moving without the presence of a propelling force.

In your teaching, you could ignore such conceptions and simply attempt to override them, submerge them or rub them out with the weight of what you say and do. The problem is that young people are likely to say they agree with you (it always pays to be agreeable because the teacher leaves you alone) while secretly maintaining and using what they really think. It can help to find out what they think and work on it. There are several ways of doing this. You could simply ask some questions at the outset: 'We eat food. What do plants do?' and encourage pupils to express their ideas so you understand them. What do you do then? Here are some possibilities.

- When there is a prevalent conception, such as 'balloons filled with air float away', you may be able to contradict it immediately. Here, you could have some pupils blow up balloons and release them. When this is not possible, you may refute it by argument or by using an explanation in a book, particularly when this reminds pupils of something they already know.
- You could help pupils make predictions from their ideas that are either obviously untrue or can be shown to be so. For instance, all stones sink (pupil law); this is a stone (pumice) so it will sink (prediction) but it floats (contradiction). If competing conceptions are expressed, you may be able to have the pupils test them practically themselves.
- After such work, you could ask older, more able pupils to construct a multiple-choice question designed to catch those who hold different conceptions (Hein, 1999).

Confronting a misconception in several different ways is more effective than relying on one approach alone (Newton, 2005).

Task 1.5   In the heat of the moment

Your pupils tell you that, 'When the Sun shines on the Bunsen burner flame, it makes the flame weaker.'

Why might pupils think this way? List some reasons.

How would you respond? Discuss your ideas with your tutor or a colleague.

Task 1.6   Diagnosing alternative conceptions

Finding out what your pupils think by questioning them can take time. The discussion can be worth it, but some teachers find pencil and paper tests quicker. This is an example of a question to elicit pupils' ideas about weight in a vacuum (Tsai and Chou, 2002).

Here, on the Earth, this block of wood weighs 10kg. It is covered by a bell jar and then the air is removed. What will happen to the weight of the wood?

A   It will weigh nothing.
B   It will weigh much less than 10kg but more than nothing.
C   It will weigh 10kg.
D   It will weigh more than 10kg.

I think this because:

(i)   Taking the air out lets the block of wood lift up quite a lot.
(ii)   Taking the air out lets the block of wood lift up a little.
(iii)   Taking the air out makes no detectable difference.
(iv)   Taking the air out lets the block sag down.

Task 1.6 *continued*

Construct a multiple choice question for the conception described in Task 1.5. If possible, try it out on a class. Otherwise, compare your question with those of colleagues and, hence, refine it.

MODELS OF SCIENCE TEACHING AND CONCEPTIONS OF LEARNING

How will you become a better teacher? Planning ahead, thinking about what you will do, anticipating problems, and reflecting on what went well and not so well after a lesson can all help enormously. But you can also learn a lot from models of teaching, or at least some of them. Here are some models of teaching:

- *books and films* about school life, such as Thomas Hughes' *Tom Brown's Schooldays* (1857) and Roald Dahl's *Matilda* (1996);
- *experienced teachers*, for example, those who taught you and those you observe;
- *others* like yourself;
- *school textbooks*.

Fiction is generally not a good starting point because it may reflect neither current practice nor pupil behaviour, if it ever did. Experienced teachers, on the other hand, do provide you with real models of practice but not always for the better. There is evidence that we tend to begin by teaching as we were taught ourselves (Moallem, 1998). If our past teachers were not examples of good practice, this may not be a good thing. But there are experienced science teachers around you who are familiar with current expectations and do things well. Others like yourself, just beginning a teaching career, can also have useful skills and ideas.

Task 1.7 Ghosts from the past

Think about your science teaching. Have you done things the way you were taught when you were at school?

1   Think of a specific way of explaining something that stems from your past experience of education.

2   Think of a general approach to your science teaching that draws on your past experience of education.

These may or may not be models of good practice. What is your view? If you consider one or the other or both to be good practice, what makes it/them good? Write a note recording your view and keep it in your file. Return to the note towards the end of your course to see if your ideas change or develop.

Task 1.8 Contemporary models

Think about one or two teachers you work with who do some part of their job well. State clearly what it is they *do* that makes their work effective.

1

2

3

Could you make these actions a part of your repertoire? Incorporate one or more of the actions in a lesson plan and, if possible, try them out for yourself.

Textbooks are sometimes referred to as surrogate teachers. This means they play the part of a teacher and attempt to support learning (Newton, 1990). They have often been written by very experienced teachers and so offer you that experience as lesson introductions, explanations, analogies, activities and exercises. A good book should suggest what might be in your lesson, what its structure might be, how it might be approached, what questions are important, and how you might explain without your words simply going over the pupils' heads. The key words here, of course, are 'a good book'. A good book is, amongst other things, one that covers what is required, presses the pupils to think about it, helps them understand the topic and apply what they learn. Some of these things are easier to gauge than others. You will soon know if a book does the topic you want, but how well does it support understanding? Many books emphasise the acquisition of information so that understanding is secondary. A useful rule of thumb in judging support for understanding is to look for the number of times the book offers and asks for reasons, purposes and causes. If they are few, the book may not be a good model of teaching for understanding.

Task 1.9 Judging textbooks as models

Contrast the following textbook accounts of hydrogen. Which is likely to be the better teaching model?

Account A: 'Hydrogen is the first element of the periodic table. It is the lightest element and is diatomic, colourless and odourless. In our world, it generally only occurs combined with other elements.'

Account B: 'Think of the elements in the periodic table. The lightest is a gas called hydrogen. A shoebox would only need about ½g of hydrogen to fill it if it was at the same temperature and pressure as in your classroom. This is because molecules of hydrogen are small and well spaced out. You could get more into the box if you squashed it in. Why is that possible? There is plenty of hydrogen in the world but you won't find much hydrogen gas floating around. This is because it is so light, it easily escapes into space. It is also quite reactive so what is left is tied up with other elements to form compounds, like water. Can you name an element that hydrogen combines with? Why did you choose that one?'

List your reasons for choosing A or B. Compare the reasons with those of colleagues. For a topic of your choice, prepare an explanation using your preferred model as a guide. If possible, try it out.

SUMMARY

Science sets out to explain the natural world; it demands empirical evidence and its ideas may change if the evidence demands it. This process has produced robust knowledge. Explanations that are not open to question or subject to empirical evidence are not scientific explanations. Science for all is generally considered to be a good thing because science has distinctive, powerful ways of thinking and working, it offers well-founded understandings, and it has the potential to contribute to the economy. By necessity, science education must be selective and its content also changes with views of scientific literacy.

Pupils often bring with them conceptions of science and scientists. These conceptions, amongst other things, help to shape how the pupils respond to science lessons. But pupils can also have conceptions of specific aspects of science. Some of these may impede learning and you need to address them in your teaching. How you teach may draw on models of teaching from the past and the present. Probably no model is perfect, even if you are sure of what that means. Nevertheless, models may suggest useful and effective ways of working that could save you time.

Task 1.10   A problem to solve: a time to sow and a time to plant

Scenario

Roger's Key Stage 3 work this term with a new class included teaching about local plants. He examined a couple of textbooks and found that they simply described habitats, niches, diversity, the animals that depended on the plants and threats to them – there were no ideas for investigations. Roger put the books aside and made a list of a few problems he would set his class to solve:

Week 1: What plants are out there?
Week 2: Why do some plants grow in some places but not in others?
Week 3: What lives on them? What would happen if one kind of plant disappeared?

In the first lesson of each week, he wrote the problem on the board and divided the class into pairs of pupils who planned how they would answer the question. In the second lesson of each week, the pairs examined plants on the school's premises. In Week 4 he gave the class a test and was horrified at the responses. His pupils could name a few more plants than before but they believed that where plants grew was a matter of luck, bees 'ate' flowers, and if a plant species disappeared 'the place would just look different'. They also said they were bored.

Where might Roger have gone wrong?

Could the books have been useful after all? What would you do?

Task 1.10 *continued*

What misconceptions (alternative conceptions) were present or developed during the activities? How would you address them?

Share your thoughts with a colleague or a tutor.

After you have solved the problem, and for those who want a little help, there are some brief notes on page 94.

FURTHER READING

ASE (Association for Science Education) (2006) *Science Education in Schools: issues, evidence and proposals*, Hatfield: ASE. An account of the ASE's view of science education in the future.

Newton, D.P. (2000) *Teaching for Understanding*, London: RoutledgeFalmer. Chapter 8 describes alternative/misconceptions and ways of addressing them in the classroom.

Reiss, M. (2005) 'The nature of science', in J. Frost and T. Turner (eds), *Learning to Teach Science in the Secondary School: a companion to school experience*, 2nd edn, Abingdon: RoutledgeFalmer, 44–53. A fuller account of the nature of science, and the companion volume to this book.

Wolpert, L. (1993) *The Unnatural Nature of Science*, London: Faber and Faber. Wolpert offers a very readable account of the nature of science.

The LearnNet website is also a useful source. For instance, it describes the use of concept cartoons to support thinking about investigations, available on: www.chem.soc.org/networks/learnnet/w-cartoons.htm/.

Chapter 2   **Preparing to teach science**

Planning for learning

I learned very early the difference between knowing something and knowing the name of something.
Richard Feynman

INTRODUCTION

We now move from what underpins your teaching to preparing to teach. The purpose of this chapter is to help you achieve the kind of learning you want to see in your lessons and to do so safely. By the end of the chapter you should be able to:

- bring your scientific and pedagogical knowledge up to scratch in readiness to plan and teach;
- distinguish kinds of learning in science;
- draw up lesson plans;
- make provision to catch the interest of pupils;
- take into account the need for a safe environment.

Task 2.1 is a warm-up activity.

Task 2.1 Mr/Ms Know-it-all?

Teachers have said that you never really know anything until you have to teach it. But, surely, you must know your subject by now. After all, you've been through what your pupils have to learn, and more, so how can this be true?

Discuss this with colleagues or a tutor.

YOUR SCIENTIFIC AND PEDAGOGICAL KNOWLEDGE

Everyone will tell you that you need to know your subject to teach it. You can't argue with that; subject knowledge helps you plan, explain, discuss, ask relevant questions, answer questions and digress usefully. It also gives you confidence and fluency in your teaching (Leinhardt *et al.*, 1991; Carlsen, 1991). The problem is that there is a lot of science out there.

You may have specialised in a relatively narrow part of it while other parts are a little rusty. Even if you know your science well, most teachers need to widen their knowledge of the parts they have to teach. Science teachers are not alone in this. History teachers, for instance, may not have studied the particular period they have to teach. Similarly, English teachers may not know this year's set book. And, of course, syllabuses change so your knowledge may have to be extended from time to time. At the same time, you need to develop your pedagogical knowledge. Amongst other things, this involves knowing effective ways of explaining things, knowing activities that help pupils grasp ideas or gain new skills, and knowing how you will manage your class in a given room (Hollon *et al.*, 1991).

You will have observed skilful teachers who do not seem to plan their lessons. Don't be deceived: what you see is the accumulated knowledge and skill that comes with practice so that, now, these teachers have their plans in their heads. They got there by slowly widening their subject knowledge and, at the same time, developing their stock of explanations, activities, ways of working and illustrative anecdotes. You could, of course, use a process of trial and error but this is likely to be slow and painful. A more efficient, time-saving way is to develop your knowledge by drawing on the resources around you. One that can offer significant support is a model of science teaching, such as a school textbook (mentioned in Chapter 1). You may also be able to seek advice from a mentor or another experienced science teacher. For instance, he or she will be able to advise you on activities that match the resources. Teachers, however, are often busy and it is unfair to go to them without having done some of the work yourself. You could begin with the pupils' textbook. Textbook writers, usually teachers themselves, have taken time to collect ideas, organise them and apply their knowledge of learners *at a level suited to the pupils you teach*. This helps you over several hurdles by giving you:

- the science knowledge you need to be sure of;
- the kind of work appropriate for your pupils;
- some activities you might use;
- a learning sequence so that your lessons hang together and go somewhere;
- everyday examples of the science;
- explanations and analogies.

Just talking about things is better than nothing, but giving the pupils some kind of experience of what you want them to learn is generally better. Experience can be obtained in several different ways. First, there is a *demonstration* in which pupils watch you do something, such as extract a metal by reduction with carbon or use a microscope. Second, there is *hands-on* experience in which pupils try it for themselves, as when they rub an eraser vigorously and find that it becomes warm, or practise a skill, as in focusing a microscope to see plant cells. A third kind of direct experience is the *investigation* in which pupils test ideas practically to develop knowledge and investigative skills, as when they investigate the effect of object shape on terminal velocity in free-fall. Generally, such activities take place in school but fieldwork is an opportunity for the pupils to study authentic contexts, as when they carry out comparative surveys of plant life in different environments using sampling devices like quadrats (see also Frost, 2005 and Turner, 2005a). With direct experience, be sure the activities have been assessed for safety. Also make sure that the pupils are clear about the purpose of the activity. Ask them: Why are you doing it? What is it for?

From time to time, you also provide indirect experience. This could be through a picture (such as one showing the heart or an industrial, fractional distillation column), a model (of, for instance, the eye or a complex molecule), a television programme or similar presentation (showing, for example, a hospital ultrasound machine), or a computer simulation (as in an animated depiction of radioactive decay to show the meaning of half-life). As with direct experience, try things out before the lesson to make sure they run smoothly. Do not assume that pupils will do your job for you while you sit and watch: they will need your support. Again make sure the pupils are clear about the purpose. Stop a television presentation at key points and ask for a review. Have them predict what might happen next.

Task 2.2 Using a model of teaching (Key Stage 3)

In this activity, practise working quickly and efficiently.

Choose one of the Key Stage 3 topics from the table below, preferably one you feel least sure about. Next, choose one or two Key Stage 3 textbooks and use these as sources of subject knowledge (the science knowledge you would need to teach) and pedagogical knowledge (for example, easy to understand explanations, everyday examples, introductory activities, investigations, things for the pupils to think about or discuss). You should, of course, use your own knowledge to supplement what you find and you can draw on other sources. (NB: Just because an activity is in a textbook does not mean it is safe to use in school. Safety is discussed on page 27.)

Topic	Subject knowledge	Pedagogical knowledge
(a) The need for a balanced diet, *or*		
(b) How the particle theory of matter can explain the properties of materials in a solid, liquid or gaseous state, *or*		
(c) Light travels in straight lines.		

Everyday examples relating to the topic

Teachers tend to build a personal collection of useful pedagogical knowledge and examples that may not be in textbooks. Your tutor's thoughts on your collection could be useful, particularly regarding matters of safety.

Task 2.3 Using a model of teaching (Key Stage 4)

Again, practise working quickly and efficiently.

Choose one of the Key Stage 4 topics in the table below, preferably one you feel least sure about. Choose one or more Key Stage 4 textbooks and use these as sources of subject knowledge (the science knowledge you would need to teach) and pedagogical knowledge (for example, easy to understand explanations,

Task 2.3 *continued*

everyday examples, introductory activities, investigations, things for the pupils to think about or discuss). Use your own knowledge to supplement what you find. (NB: Just because an activity is in a textbook it does not mean it is safe to use in school. Matters of safety are discussed on page 27.)

If you are working with colleagues, you may find it useful to share ideas. Otherwise, share your ideas with your tutor.

Topic	Subject knowledge	Pedagogical knowledge
(a) The cell's nucleus as containing chromosomes that carry genes, *or*		
(b) The fractional distillation of crude oil, *or*		
(c) The reflection of waves.		

Everyday examples relating to the topic

Again, teachers often have a personal collection of useful pedagogical knowledge and examples. Your tutor's thoughts could be useful, particularly regarding matters of safety.

TRANSMITTING KNOWLEDGE OR SUPPORTING UNDERSTANDING?

You may find it useful to think of learning as collecting information and understanding it. It is possible to store large amounts of information in your head and regurgitate as needed. If this information amounted to telephone numbers and names, there's not much more you could do with it. As elsewhere, science has its facts to learn. But, what we talk about in science is often underpinned by reasons, purposes and causes. With these, explanations can make sense, that is, they can be understood. Understanding makes productive thinking possible (Moseley *et al.*, 2005).

Memorising

As in other subjects, there are many facts we have to remember in science. For example, we could commit to memory symbols for elements and circuit components, the colours of the rainbow, the names of bones, how to fold a filter paper, a formula relating electrical current, voltage and resistance and learn how to slot numbers in it. It's all a matter of jumping through hoops in the right order. Schools have become good at cramming in and testing this kind of information (Kusukawa and Maclean, 2006) and facts are important – without them, there is nothing to understand. So, too, are formulae and learned routines – they save time.

Understanding

Understanding is the process of making mental connections to join bits of knowledge into larger units so they make sense to us. An understanding is the result. In science, what we construct in this way is often a mental model of some part of the world. For instance, when we understand why the image in a pinhole camera is upside down, we have noticed that rays cross at the pinhole so light from the top of the object ends on the bottom of the screen and that from the bottom of the object ends on the top of the screen. This gives us the reason for (or cause of) the inverted image. Such understandings are valued as they can be very durable, they are often satisfying and motivating, and they can help us predict or explain new situations (Newton, 2000). Being able to recall facts and provide the right answer may have its satisfaction but this is nothing compared with the value of understanding. Understanding is a more flexible and useful kind of knowledge that enables more productive thought and action.

What is the problem?

Teaching for understanding is not easy. Even when you think you have explained it well and your pupils have paid attention, they may not grasp it. The problem is that you cannot give pupils your understanding. You give them parts of a jigsaw and drop big hints about how the bits join together but your pupils have to do the joining. At the same time, they have to join the bits to other jigsaws they already have in their heads (Cerbin, 2000). Add to this the possibility that pupils may arrive with a ready-made picture they have been building over several years. Their pictures may not be like the one you want and may get in the way of the new picture. Faced with this it would be easy to settle down to a routine where you give information to the pupils for them to store.

Realistically speaking

Some things have to be memorised but there is so much benefit in understanding that you should work hard at helping your pupils build it. On your part, this means you should:

- Have a small number of clear learning goals in your mind for each lesson and let the pupils know them – what precisely do you want your pupils to understand?
- Construct questions that let you (and the pupils) know that they have achieved the goals – for example, after the lesson:

    (a) they will be able to translate the explanation into their own words;
    (b) they will be able to think of new examples;
    (c) they will be able to solve this new problem;
    (d) they will be able to think critically about the control of variable x in this experiment.

- Identify and draw on prior knowledge and explain matters clearly.
- Support understanding by providing experience and structures to think with (see Chapter 3).
- Reward memorisation when that is appropriate and reward understanding when that is your goal – for example, through praise.

Always remember that you and the pupils are on the same side in this learning game. It is not simply what you do that matters or what the pupils do, but what you do together.

Task 2.4 Being clear about your goals

Choose a topic from Key Stage 3 and one from Key Stage 4 from the lists below. What would your learning goals be for most of your pupils for these topics?

Topic	I would want pupils to remember the following	I would want pupils to understand the following
Key Stage 3		
(a) The cell's nucleus as containing chromosomes that carry genes, *or*		
(b) The fractional distillation of crude oil, *or*		
(c) The reflection of waves.		
Key Stage 4		
(a) The need for a balanced diet, *or*		
(b) How the particle theory of matter can explain the properties of materials in a solid, liquid or gaseous state, *or*		
(c) Light travels in straight lines.		

Learning goals are very useful for checking on learning at the end of a lesson. All you have to do is turn the goals into questions. Try it for the goals you have listed.

CATCHING INTEREST IN SCIENCE

What is it about science that interests you? Why do you find anything interesting? The answer is that we are interested in what might satisfy some personal need. Here are some needs that might be satisfied by engaging with science:

- a need to explore the world (curiosity);
- a need for novelty (often related to the above need);
- a need to feel competent (stemming from knowledge, understandings and skills);
- a need for affiliation (relating successfully with others);
- a need for autonomy (the 'I did it my way' need).

Science that clearly relates to a personal need is likely to be perceived as interesting. Science you tie to a need that is felt now is likely to be more attractive than science that relates to a need pupils may have in the future. Science related directly to the pupils or their friends or family tends to be more attractive than that related to vague groups of people elsewhere, although interest in the latter may never be absent and may grow with time. Each of these relates science to people, individually or collectively, so science involves products, processes and people. When we teach science, it is easy to ignore the people dimension, but interest can stem from it and interest is motivating so it is worth your attention.

This means you should look for connections between the topic you have to teach and people. Here are some examples:

- When teaching about microbes, you might tell the pupils about the world's largest known bacterium. It is half a millimetre long and can just be seen by the naked eye. It would take only twenty of them to make a centimetre of bugs. (*Epulopiscium fishelsoni* lives in the gut of fish in the Red Sea and was discovered in 1985.)
- When teaching about plants and their diversity, you might ask what it could have been like way back in time, when plants first colonised the land. The fossil evidence suggests that the first land plants were of the liverwort kind. You could show them a picture of a liverwort or, better, a live specimen in situ.
- When looking at the properties of materials, you may remind pupils of 'toys' like pots of 'goo' and power balls, and talk about materials with memories for which the pupils think of sensible and crazy uses.
- Instead of introducing a lesson with, 'Today we are going to look at the oxidation of iron', you might begin by telling the pupils how iron cannon-balls in shipwrecks become encrusted with sand and organic materials. When they are brought to the surface in the open air and the encrustation is knocked off, they sometimes become red hot (*New Scientist*, 2002, no. 2342). Why? You might then make the point by showing how readily steel wool burns (Newton, 2005).
- When teaching about the way water expands when it is heated, you might talk about how global warming will not only melt the ice caps but will also make the sea level rise further owing to the expansion of water. Also in connection with heat, you could ask how we might keep houses cool, given the likelihood of very hot summers. You could mention special paints designed to reflect a significant amount of the sun's radiation.
- When introducing the topic of electricity, pupils may list its uses in everyday life to demonstrate its importance.
- When teaching about magnetism, tell the pupils how people use to believe that rubbing a magnet with garlic destroyed its powers. Ask how they would test the idea. Ask them to comment on a school catalogue advertisement for magnets that says, 'Suitable for use on all metal-based surfaces.' How would they rewrite the advertisement?
- When teaching about Newton's Third Law (every action has an equal and opposite reaction), you could ask the pupils what a snowball fight in space would be like. Tell

them that each astronaut has a bag of snowballs and they begin in a circle facing each other.

You might use some of these ideas to start a lesson. Others might be integrated into a lesson while some might be used to round a lesson off. You can begin by pointing out the relevance of the topic for pupils personally or for society at large and sometimes you may be able to use a recent event or news report. But guard against justifying everything by its practical

---

Task 2.5 Science with added interest

Where is the interest in these topics? Describe potential sources of interest for the following. You may find it helps if you ask yourself, 'Why is this topic important?' You may also find it useful to consult a variety of sources, including colleagues with specialist knowledge and more general books about science for young people. Some ideas may lead to safe, practical investigations and are more useful because of that. You may find it easier to begin with the aspect of science that most interests you.

Key Stage 3 topics	Potential source of interest
(a) The role of the skeleton.	
(b) Separating mixtures using chromatography.	
(c) The appearance of coloured objects in light of various colours.	

Key Stage 4 topics	Potential source of interest
(a) The basic principles of cloning.	
(b) Addition polymers.	
(c) How to determine the speed of an object.	

Begin a database of ideas, anecdotes and everyday instances of science you can draw on in lesson planning.

application. Usefulness is a powerful argument but it can give you problems for those topics that do not have obvious practical applications. As Bertrand Russell said, 'There is much pleasure to be gained from useless knowledge.' And, it has to be said, there are things in science that have to be learned in order to do the interesting things (Newton, 1988). Note that knowing instances like these is a part of deepening your science knowledge. This aspect of the process may continue throughout your teaching career and can add to your own interest in teaching science.

So far, this discussion has been about making connections between the science and the pupils' needs. But there are needs that might be satisfied by the way you get pupils to work. One source of interest could stem from working together (the need for affiliation). This tends to be a well-recognised liking of pupils. Practical activity and discussion can accommodate this liking and, at the same time, can support learning. Remember, however, that affiliation can be on- or off-task, and too much of the latter can hinder learning. You can, of course, be a floating member of all groups and support their progress towards the learning goals you set.

Another source of interest, particularly for older pupils, is to allow some freedom in how they learn and present their work (a need for autonomy, Deci *et al.*, 1991). One way of doing this is to introduce the topic (including connections that are likely to generate interest), set the task and then provide a short menu of ways of doing it. For instance, you may want the pupils to learn about some medical uses of hormones and so you give them a menu, such as:

Present what you find, either:

1 as half a page of writing (you can include diagrams);
2 as a mind or concept map on an A3 sheet of paper;
3 as a storyboard (like a serious cartoon strip) on an A3 sheet of paper.

Other ideas include, for instance, making and explaining (orally) a model and preparing a Powerpoint-like presentation. You may need to explain what you mean by some of these and the time constraints if the pupils are not familiar with this way of working. You should not, of course, let the pupils continually avoid one way of working, especially when it is the norm for responses in external examinations.

Needs vary from person to person so what interests you may not interest your pupils and what interests one pupil may not interest another. Although you may not catch everyone's interest all the time, you should try to catch most pupils' interest a lot of the time and, with variety, catch everyone's interest fairly regularly.

Task 2.6 'I did it my way'

Provide menus for work in one or more of the following topics at Key Stage 4 (or for a topic you will teach soon):

(a) A summary of the impact of humans on the environment.
(b) An account of what the periodic table tells us.
(c) An account of an investigation into the effect of chemical concentration on the rate of reaction.
(d) How energy is transferred from power stations to consumers.

Add these to your collection (e.g. a database) of 'bright ideas' for future use in lesson planning.

PRODUCTIVE, SAFE SCIENCE LESSONS

Safety

It would be difficult, probably impossible, to meet the requirements of the National Curriculum for Science without the pupils doing some hands-on practical work. You have to take reasonable care for the safety of your pupils, yourself and other adults in your workplace. This means you should:

- think ahead and anticipate potential safety problems;
- follow the safety advice provided by bodies such as CLEAPSS (Consortium of Local Education Authorities for the Provision of Science Services);
- adhere to the requirements regarding safety and activities in your school's science scheme of work or its equivalent;
- observe the recommendations, guidelines, rules and regulations of your employer;
- keep safety equipment to hand;
- be an example of good practice yourself;
- report deficiencies and defects likely to adversely affect safety.

Because science teachers do these, accidents in science laboratories amount to only 2 per cent of all reported accidents in schools (most occur in PE, games, the playground and in corridors) (CLEAPSS, 2004).

Task 2.7 A preliminary checklist

When preparing to teach science, you should be aware of some matters to do with safety. Below is a list of some of the more important ones. Tick them as you find out about each one, perhaps with the help of your tutor.

- ☐ The school's science safety policy.
- ☐ The location of the mains gas tap.
- ☐ The mains electricity switch.
- ☐ The fire alarm and collection point.
- ☐ The location of fire extinguishers and blankets, and their use.
- ☐ The correct operation of devices such as fume cupboards.
- ☐ The location and use of a chemical spill kit.
- ☐ The first aid kit, eye wash, and identity of the first aider.
- ☐ The reporting procedure should an accident occur, including one to yourself.
- ☐ The safety precautions associated with activities you will teach in the science department's scheme of work.

Keep a record of this activity in your teaching experience file. Add any useful information on safety you collect, for future use.

How do you take reasonable care that what you plan is likely to be safe? First, the activities in the science schemes of work your school has prepared should have been checked for safety. That is, the risk associated with each should have been assessed, often in relation to nationally available model risk assessments. What you should do regarding safety will be stated, appended, or otherwise made available. Your part is to follow that advice. Should you want to do an activity that has not been assessed in this way or is a variant of one in the scheme of work, a risk assessment must be made. To do this, you have to consider 'how likely it is that something will go wrong and how serious the consequences would be' then put in place safety precautions 'to reduce the risk from any hazard to an acceptable level' (CLEAPSS, 2004). To begin with, it is better to do this in conjunction with a more experienced colleague who is familiar with the process. Such a lesson plan must be checked by a class teacher (as are all your lesson plans). In some circumstances, external advice, such as from CLEAPSS, may need to be sought in accordance with the employer's instructions. Remember that you should take into account how your pupils tend to behave, the class size, your class control skills and your own level of practical competence. Also bear in mind that you may not work so proficiently in an unfamiliar laboratory as you would in one where you know exactly where everything is.

In addition to your concern about the safety of laboratory work, you should expect pupils to develop a similar concern. Teach them how to work safely, have them practise identifying potential hazards and gauge and reduce risks in ways that suit their age, experience and ability. Remember that a field trip and its associated activities are subject to the same requirements as indoor laboratory activities.

A brief account of matters to do with safety, such as this, cannot provide you with the detail you need for particular activities. You should follow the guidance and instructions provided in school and in documents on safety.

Task 2.8   Learn more about safe practices in the laboratory

There are several sources of information about safety and school science teaching. For example, there is the ASE's *Safeguards in the School Laboratory* (see Further Reading) and 'Health and Safety in the School Laboratory and the new Science Teacher' available at www.cleapss.org.uk. The CLEAPSS *Hazcards* give more specific guidance on safety.

By yourself or with a colleague, use such sources to compile a list of *general* risks in school laboratories.

Now consider your list. How would you use it to involve your pupils directly in matters of safety?

Transitions

Science lessons often involve transitions from one activity to another. Here are a few:

- 'Stop what you are doing and pay attention. We need to do the next bit.'
- 'Gather around the front bench so I can show you this.'
- 'Bring your stools around the television.'
- 'Collect a test tube and test tube holder from the side bench.'
- 'Put everything away and tidy up. When everything is tidy, come to the front and we'll talk about what you found.'
- 'OK. That's the bell. End of lesson.'

If transitions are badly managed, they can get in the way of learning. For example, if your pupils are working productively on an account of an investigation, an interruption by you for something that could wait may be an unnecessary distraction. Transitions may also provide opportunities for unwanted behaviour. This takes time to deal with, it attracts the attention of others and it may affect safety.

How do you deal with transitions? The trick is:

1 Identify them in your lesson plan and minimise their impact by avoiding unnecessary transitions.
2 Devise simple routines for the pupils to follow. Your science department may already use effective routines so take advantage of them. Otherwise, devise your own and use them consistently so they become habits. For example, you need a routine for collecting and returning equipment to avoid it becoming a free-for-all. One teacher tended to have pupils work in pairs. One of each pair formed a queue to collect certain items from one bench while the other joined another queue for the remaining items on another bench. Although the pupils always needed supervision, they learned the routine quickly.
3 Think twice about interrupting safe, productive activity.

Task 2.9 Managing transitions

Either choose a lesson from the topics listed in Task 2.4 *or* choose one you will soon teach. Set out an *outline* lesson plan on the proforma below. Identify the necessary transitions. Describe how you will deal with them. Discuss your ideas with your tutor.

Topic	Key Stage/class	Duration

Key Science Knowledge

Everyday examples and other sources of interest

'By the end of the lesson' goals

(a) The pupils should know:

Task 2.9 *continued*

Topic	Key Stage/class	Duration

(b) The pupils should understand:

(c) The pupils should be able to:

**Lesson agenda (sequence
of main teaching events,
including activities)**

Safety matters to be checked

Transitions involved

SUMMARY

Your scientific knowledge matters but no one knows it all. Your aim is to widen your knowledge of what you teach and add interesting connections, such as everyday examples that make the relevance of science explicit. You also need, of course, to include ways of teaching the science effectively. There are various sources of such knowledge and one that is readily available is the textbook. Some aspects of science are of the 'need to know' kind but understanding is highly valued because it ties knowledge together in a meaningful way, it is potentially flexible and it is durable. You cannot *give* someone an understanding, but you can help them develop an understanding by what you do and what you say.

It is your duty to attend to matters of safety in the laboratory. You should follow the school's rules and regulations and be familiar with safety precautions and procedures. Take advice from more experienced colleagues and keep up to date with the safety literature. Lessons involve transitions between activities. These need to be planned to maintain a safe and purposeful learning environment.

Task 2.10 A problem to solve: the best laid plans

Mr Ward had taught successfully for many years and his pupils always got good examination results, which pleased the headteacher and the parents. He was always aware, however, that there was more to teaching and learning than cramming the pupils' minds with knowledge and setting examination questions until they came

Task 2.10 *continued*

out of their ears. He decided to change his approach and so put together a unit he called *Sight and Light*. His plan was for the pupils to arrive at some of the principles of light by their practical investigation of photography.

He was not happy with the outcome. First, some pupils knew a bit about photography while others did not. Several sessions were spent getting everyone to the same point and some lost interest. After that, the principles they discovered were fragmentary and lacked coherence. When he gave the end of unit test, which he had constructed to test the pupils' ability to apply knowledge in new situations, the pupils did very badly. As this was an optional element of the curriculum, they left in large numbers (Wallace and Louden, 2003).

Analyse the situation. What could be the cause(s) of the problem?

Could the approach be saved and given a chance of working? Construct a less risky approach that would help the pupils construct understandings while keeping an eye on examination requirements.

After you have solved the problem, and for those who want a little help, there are some brief notes on page 94.

FURTHER READING

ASE (Association for Science Education) (2006a) *Safeguards in the School Laboratory*, Hatfield: ASE. This is a standard handbook on safety in the laboratory. Always use the latest edition.

Newton, D.P. (2000) *Teaching for Understanding*, London: RoutledgeFalmer. For a fuller account of the nature of understanding, see Chapters 2–4.

Newton, D.P. (2005) 'Motivating students in science', in L.D. Newton (ed.) *Meeting the Standards in Secondary Science*, London: Routledge. This offers a short account of motivation in science education with some specific examples of how to interest pupils.

Youens, B. (2005) 'Planning and evaluating lessons', in J. Frost and T. Turner, *Learning to Teach Science in the Secondary School: a companion to school experience*, 2nd edn, Abingdon: RoutledgeFalmer, 125–40. Chapter 5 gives further details of planning should you need it.

Chapter 3 Teaching

Supporting scientific thinking in the classroom

The teacher should never lose his temper in the presence of a class. If a man, he may take refuge in profane soliloquies; if a woman, she may . . . go out in the yard and gnaw a post.

William Phelps

INTRODUCTION

Most of us want to be the kind of teacher who really engages the pupils in science and makes them want more. What should you do? According to your pupils, you should be enthusiastic, make the topic interesting, be willing to listen to and use their ideas, help them understand, show you care about their learning, be approachable and provide help at the individual level (Darby, 2005). Well, you have planned your lesson and now you have to turn it into words and actions. This means you have to think on your feet. The purpose of this chapter is to help you do some of the things the pupils value. By the end of the chapter you should:

- know some ways that help pupils remember and understand;
- know how to scaffold thought through, for example, questions, bridges, and analogies; and
- know when words could be a problem and what to do about it.

Task 3.1 gives you a flavour of what many pupils value in a lesson.

Task 3.1 Did you make 'em think today?

Here, thinking refers to what it takes to produce:

- ideas and solutions to problems, as when seeking a way to control a variable;
- explanations, reasons, justifications and predictions, as when a pupil tells you why something happens as it did, justifies a procedure, or tells you what will happen;
- clarifications by, for instance, expanding upon an explanation or plan of action;
- paraphrases, as when rewording the explanations of others;
- evaluations, as in pointing to weaknesses in an argument, investigation, procedure or evidence.

Task 3.1 *continued*

Think about a recent lesson that went fairly well and tick the appropriate box for each item below. (Note that there are items for your contribution and items for the pupils' contribution – you are in this together.)

0 = not like this lesson; 1 = a little like this lesson, 2 = definitely like this lesson; 3 = very like this lesson

	0	1	2	3

Your side of things:

1 You asked for the pupils' prior knowledge and tried to use it. ☐☐☐☐

2 You asked questions that pressed the pupils to think. ☐☐☐☐

3 You set tasks that required thought. ☐☐☐☐

4 You gave the pupils time to think through their answers. ☐☐☐☐

5 You involved other pupils in evaluating responses. ☐☐☐☐

6 You thought things through aloud, modelling thinking for the pupils. ☐☐☐☐

The pupils' side of things:

7 The pupils had a clear sense of what they were doing. ☐☐☐☐

8 The pupils could express your explanations in their own words. ☐☐☐☐

9 'Why?' questions were asked by pupils. ☐☐☐☐

10 Pupils came up with ideas themselves. ☐☐☐☐

11 Pupils offered explanations and reasons. ☐☐☐☐

12 Pupils spotted weaknesses in scientific thinking. ☐☐☐☐

Total score ☐

A score between:

0 and 5	Your pupils were asleep; were you?
6 and 12	A languid lesson, no great pressure on the pupils.
13 and 24	Some good attempts at thinking.
25 and 30	The lesson really made them think.
31 and 36	Teacher and pupils are firing on all cylinders.

What is more important than the total score is to note items where scores were low and target them more often. While you may try to have a reasonably high score regularly, it may be unrealistic to expect one every lesson.

Discuss with your tutor the strengths and areas for attention revealed by the list.

SHAPING THOUGHT: HELPING PUPILS REMEMBER THINGS

Attention and rehearsal

Some things just have to be committed to memory. It helps if you encourage your pupils to:

- give it attention;
- make a written note of it, as when they compile a science dictionary (Wellington and Osborne, 2001);
- practise using it in their writing and discussion; and
- relate it to something they already know or can learn easily.

Mnemonics

The last item in the list above forms the basis of the mnemonic. A mnemonic to remember the colours of the rainbow, in the order they appear (Red, Orange, Yellow, Green, Blue, Indigo, Violet) is the sentence *Richard Of York Gave Battle In Vain*. A way of remembering the classification of the animal world into Kingdom, Phylum, Class, Order, Family, Genus, Species is to remember *Kings Play Chess On Fine Grain Sand*. The order of the planets may be reconstructed from, *Many Very Elderly Men Just Snooze Under Newspapers* (relegating Pluto to the lesser planets). Mnemonics have many forms. Here is another: Veins take blood into the heart, arteries take it away from the heart. Sometimes, it may be possible to tie the facts up in a verse. Here's one about the average temperature at different times of the year:

Five, ten and twenty-one,
Winter, Spring and Summer Sun.

Pupils can find these useful (Levin *et al.*, 1986) and some go on to make their own when preparing for examinations.

Pictures

Pictures can be more memorable than words. Try to summarise the main points of a lesson in an annotated diagram. (You can frequently use such diagrams to show relationships, so pictures are discussed further below.)

Task 3.2 The trouble with facts is that there are so many of them

(a) You and your colleagues may know some useful science mnemonics. Make a collection.

Task 3.2 *continued*

(b) Many pupils today would not find the ROYGBIV mnemonic above any more memorable than having to recall the colours themselves in the right order. They need one drawn from something they know well in their world. Can you devise one? If you work with a colleague, you may find that your thoughts are more productive.

SHAPING THOUGHT: HELPING PUPILS THINK PRODUCTIVELY

Pictures

Mental working space has its limits. Working with new ideas or several things at once can push it to the limit. When this happens, your job is to reduce the burden to what is manageable. So, for instance, you might turn to the board and provide a *diagram* that represents the carbon cycle or summarises the process of photosynthesis, or makes the path of a light ray through a lens easier to follow. Diagrams are pictures that have been simplified to show what matters. They capture, relate and summarise a lot of information and can be more memorable than words (the 'a picture is worth a thousand words' effect). Annotated diagrams are also used to store information as a kind of memory extension. For example, you may ask for potential explanations of rusting and present them in a diagram called a concept cartoon (Keogh and Naylor, 1999). Figure 3.1, for instance, keeps the explanations in view to support

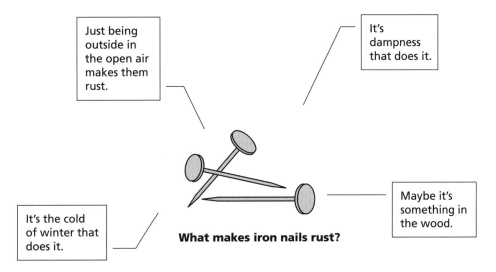

Figure 3.1 What makes iron nails rust? An *aide memoire* for pupils' ideas

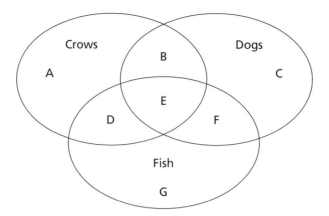

Figure 3.2 A chart to aid comparison

investigation planning and drawing of a conclusion. Other diagrams require the pupil to work on them. For instance, you might want pupils to compare certain living things on their way to learning about taxonomic groups. You could give them a chart like that in figure 3.2. A, C, and G are for differences between the animals. B, D and F are for characteristics they share. E is for what is common to all of them. Charts like this reduce mental load and help pupils manage the task.

To help pupils grasp the meaning of written materials, there are activities known as DARTs (Directed Activities Related to Text). For instance, pupils might be given a diagram without labels. They have to read and hence provide the labels. Similarly, an explanation about a topic may have words missing or sentences in the wrong order and pupils supply the words or order the sentences after reading (Frost, 2005: 183). Diagrams can, of course, be a learning or assessment exercise as when a picture of the carbon cycle is given to pupils in pieces for them to assemble and turn into words.

Task 3.3   Doing it with pictures

Construct a simple diagram to help you explain:

- the digestive system; *or*
- a car's catalytic converter; *or*
- multiple echoes heard on a boat on a lake amongst mountains.

Task 3.3 *continued*

Construct a chart to help pupils see similarities and differences in:

- plant cells and animal cells; *or*
- light and sound; *or*
- the properties of sodium and potassium and calcium.

Explain to a colleague why your chart and diagram will help pupils understand. If possible, try them out on pupils.

Prompts and questions

Perhaps more common is the help you provide by what you say. See yourself as providing a *scaffold* to support and shape pupils' thoughts rather than as someone who simply tells pupils the answers. At its simplest, you would gently prompt pupils who are losing their way in their explanations. So, when a pupil tries to explain what she found when she varied the voltage across various electrical components, the conversation might be:

Pupil: 'That one, there, the current went up the same each time.'
You: 'Each time?'
Pupil: 'When the voltage went up the same amount each time. We went up in 2 volts each time.'
You: 'What about that one?'
Pupil: 'No, that didn't work.'
You: 'Didn't work?'
Pupil: 'It worked, sort of. It went up more to start with then less at the end.'
. . . etc.

Interaction like this is important. You support individual pupils, it helps them think and organise their thoughts and it acknowledges their progress.

Task 3.4   Guiding thought

How would you support this pupil's thinking? What would you say?

Topic: *Magnetism: the compass*, Key Stage 3.

Teacher: 'So, which end of the compass points north?'
Pupil: 'That end.'
Teacher: 'Which end is that?'
Pupil: [Hesitation.] 'It's wrong.'
Teacher: 'Oh, why?'
Pupil: 'It's supposed to be the south end that's attracted to the North Pole.'
Teacher: ?

You may find it helpful to work with a colleague if that is possible. Work on your own first then compare responses.

This introduces *questions*. Questioning has a large part in scaffolding thought but your questions have to be the right ones. For example, anyone who has had pupils work with simple circuits knows that dealing with circuit faults can stall your lesson. The trick is to teach pupils to find and correct faults themselves. *Focused questioning* takes pupils through the stages of understanding to a simple, fault-finding routine.

1 Set the scene and show relevance. (*Did you see the news about the power cut? Is it important? Why? What made the power go off?*)
2 Bring out relevant prior knowledge. (*Do you know how a torch works? Can you tell me? Who wants to start us off?*) If sound, spread the knowledge about, make sure everyone is at the same starting point; if unsound, take remedial action (immediately if it is important for what follows).
3 Focus on what matters; deflect attention from what does not matter. (*This torch doesn't work. I wonder why. Any ideas? Let's take it apart and have a look.*)
4 Have them think things through. (*How can we test the battery? How can we test the bulb? What if it's a faulty wire? How can we test a wire? What's a good way of working? One thing at a time? Why?*)
5 Pull the key points together. (*So, what do you do if your circuit doesn't work? First, check the . . .? How will you do that? Then check the . . .? How will you do that? etc. Step by step! That's what counts. What counts? etc.*)

Note that the teacher in the above example asked 'why' questions. Her aim was to have the pupils develop a systematic way of working with circuits *and* understand why that worked. This kind of knowledge is more flexible and durable than simply learning a procedure by heart.

There is, however, another kind of question that can help pupils construct an understanding: *forced prediction*. Even when pupils have information, they may remain passive with it. If you ask them to make a prediction, they must focus on and process the information to see the pattern and make sense of it (Newton, 1994). Only then can they answer your question. For example, when you explain the function of the parts of a leaf, you might then ask, 'What would happen if we covered the underside of a leaf with cling film?'

Task 3.5   Pressing for understanding

Focused questions

Think of the questions you might ask when you are teaching about:

- *feeding relationships in an ecosystem:* the pupils cut out pictures of animals and plants that form a community and arrange them into a pyramidal web; *or*
- *electrolysis:* the pupils electroplate a suitable metal with copper; *or*
- *electromagnetic induction:* the pupils use a coil and magnet to generate transient currents in a galvanometer.

Think of a question that:

- sets the scene and shows relevance:

- brings out relevant prior knowledge:

- focuses on what matters:

- has them think things through:

- pulls key points together:

Forced prediction

Construct a forced prediction question you might ask during or after you have completed your focused questioning.

Check the science first then discuss your responses (questions) with your tutor or colleagues.

Bridges

There is often a gap between what your pupils know and can do and where you want them to go next. *Bridging* helps them cross that gap. You construct steps so that moving from one to the next is not too demanding. Often, these steps involve practical activities. For instance, suppose you had to teach about condensation with some younger pupils. Some steps might be:

1 You ask them what they think the word means and if they have seen condensation before. You might ask when condensation is more likely.
2 You show small, plastic bottles of cold water with a mist developing on the outside and droplets forming. You tell pupils the aim of the lesson, namely, to see if you and they can work out what made these bottles wet.
3 You ask what the dampness is and several guess it is water. You show that anhydrous copper sulphate changes from white to blue when water touches it. They try it on the mist and show it is likely to be water.
4 You ask where this water has come from. Is it soaking through the walls of the bottle? Where else might it come from? You collect ideas and help them design tests. Is the water level falling in the bottle? If they keep air off the bottle with a cloth, does that stop mist forming?
5 You ask, can there be water in the air? You point out that puddles disappear and they breathe out water vapour.
6 You ask when it is easier to see the water in the air and draw their attention to cold days and breathing. 'So,' you ask, 'do we know now why these bottles are wet?' You go on to elicit the generalisation that air gives up some of its water when it cools.
7 Now you ask them to predict what would happen if they filled bottles with warm water. After they have justified their prediction, it is tested.
8 Finally, you bring it all together, and have them apply their new knowledge to explain why it is more likely to be misty at night than during the day.

Note that the steps involved direct experience, that what you say focuses attention on what matters and guides thinking.

Task 3.6 Bridge building

Construct a bridge to support the understanding of:

- asexual reproduction; *or*
- rate of reaction; *or*
- temperature.

The bridge can have as many steps as you feel is helpful and may include direct experience (hands-on activities) and indirect experience (for example, a picture, television presentation, a computer animation).

If possible, work in pairs on the same topic. Compare your bridge with that of another pair.

Analogies

You use an analogy when you draw parallels between what you are trying to teach and something the pupils know well or can grasp easily. Suppose you are teaching about friction between surfaces. You show how difficult it is to push the bristles of one scrubbing brush over those of another, yet how easy it is to push the back of one brush over the back of the other. To help pupils grasp the nature of friction you gave them something concrete they can see, feel and think about. We use analogies and analogy-like devices all the time (for example, 'the Earth is like an orange', 'light reflects from a mirror just like a ball bounces off a wall') and they can be important in a scientists' thought as they try to get to grips with a problem (Coll, 2005). Some analogies have become common ways of supporting understanding and it would be impossible to offer an understanding in some topics at an early stage without analogies. Take, for instance, the reflection of light: are we to draw parallels with a ball bouncing from a wall or talk of the interaction between an electromagnetic wave and the material's surface (Wallace and Louden, 2003)?

Analogies come in three kinds:

- where the analogue *looks like* what we want to teach (like the Earth, an orange is roughly spherical and has a core surrounded by a skin);
- where the analogue *behaves like* what we want to teach (the ball bounces off the wall like light reflects off a mirror);
- where the analogue *looks and behaves* like what we want to teach (water flowing in pipes is, to some extent, like an electrical current in a wire).

We tend to use the first kind almost off-the-cuff and in response to signs of incomprehension from the pupils. The second kind, however, are more powerful because they help us make predictions. For example, 'So which way will the light ray go? Think of what a ball would do.' Analogies of the third kind are powerful and memorable but are not common. Table 3.1 lists some popular analogies. They are largely of the second (e.g. the leaf is like a factory) and third kind (e.g. the eye is like a camera).

Table 3.1 Some analogies

LIFE AND LIVING PROCESSES

- *Photosynthesis* The leaf is like a factory which takes in bottles of carbon dioxide and water and, with energy from its lights, makes bags of sugar which are stored in the warehouse.
- *The eye* The eye is like a camera with its lens, stop (iris), and light sensitive surface (film or electronic light sensor).
- *Homeostasis* Homeostasis is similar to what we try to do with central heating; we try to keep the temperature at a steady level with the help of a thermostat.
- *DNA molecules* DNA molecules are like zip fasteners.
- *Semipermeable cell wall* The wall is like a chain link fence which only allows things of the right size and shape to pass through.

MATERIALS AND THEIR PROPERTIES

- *Compounds* Elements combine to form compounds like letters of the alphabet combine to make words.
- *Electrolytes* A non-electrolyte is like a set of assembled nuts and bolts. A strong electrolyte is like a set of unscrewed nuts and bolts. A weak electrolyte is like a set with only a few that are unscrewed.
- *Atoms* An atom is a bit like the solar system.
- *Energy levels* These are like the rungs of a ladder. You cannot stand between rungs and energy is needed to climb higher.
- *Catalyst effect* This is like avoiding climbing over the mountain tops by taking an easier way through a pass.

Table 3.1 continued

PHYSICAL PROCESSES

- *Refraction of light* Imagine wheels on an axle rolling head-on into sand. Both slow down in the sand. If the axle enters the sand at an angle, one wheel slows down more than the other. This makes the axle slew around, just like a light ray as it enters glass from the air.
- *Transmission of sound* Pulses along a slinky spring are used to show how sound travels through air. The spring is also used to show echoes as a pulse reflects from a fixed end of the spring.
- *Colour* High notes represent blue light and low notes represent red light. 'White' noise (a mix of all audible frequencies) represents white light.
- *Electrical current* Electrical current is often described in terms of water flowing through pipes.
- *Radioactive decay* The decay of some radioactive atoms is like throwing a bunch of dice over and over again and taking out the ones which come up six.

Analogies can make an explanation more memorable, they can make it more meaningful, and they can make reasoning more successful (Glynn and Takahashi, 1998; Wallace and Louden, 2003). They are not, however, without dangers. No analogy is perfect and pupils may over-extend them. The solar system is a common analogy for the atom but the parallels are not numerous and taken too far, soon mislead (Taber, 2001). At best, they trade precision for clarity, memorability and utility. And there are, of course, bad analogies. For example, 'If you took out all the oil from your head, your hair would fall out. So, if we're taking all the oil out of the Earth, then what's going to happen to it?' (*New Scientist*, 2365, 19 October 2002: 13). In higher levels of science, where there is still debate about how to explain some phenomenon, there may not even be agreement about the relevance of a particular analogy. Nevertheless, used with caution, you can 'see them as a journey towards meaning' (Heywood, 2002: 244). There are, however, some simple rules to follow:

- make sure the pupils understand the basis of the analogy – you may have to remind them of it;
- point out the parallels clearly and show how to use the analogy;
- practise using the analogy;
- point out the limitations of the analogy, and keep doing so.

Analogies can also form a step in a bridge to understanding. Pupils find difficulty believing that a table top pushes up with a force that matches the weight of the book resting on it. Many pupils believe there is only one force, namely, the weight of the book. To wean them from this, Clement (1993) had pupils compress a bed spring and feel it push back. They then compressed a sponge and saw it compressed by a book. Next, they placed the book on a thin-topped table and saw the deformation. Finally, they placed the book on a thick-topped table and detected the deformation using a mirror on the table and a ray of light reflected from it.

Task 3.7 Going to the limit

Choose three analogies, one from each group in Table 3.1.

Analogy 1

List the parallels with the target topic.

Task 3.7 *continued*

How would you have pupils apply it?

If pupils took the parallels too far, what kind of belief could it lead to?

Analogy 2

List the parallels with the target topic.

How would you have pupils apply it?

If pupils took the parallels too far, what kind of belief could it lead to?

Analogy 3

List the parallels with the target topic.

How would you have pupils apply it?

If pupils took the parallels too far, what kind of belief could it lead to?

Discuss your responses with your tutor.

THE LANGUAGE OF SCIENCE

Not all words are user-friendly. Scientific language creates an extra burden. It has a specialised vocabulary, it uses everyday words in special ways, it has a liking for strange expressions and it is not like the language we use in our conversations. It can be overwhelming for a novice so it is not surprising that Frost (2005) describes learning science as learning a new language. What can you do to help? Look at it in two parts: first, there is the problem of grasping the meaning of non-specialised English and, second, there are the specific problems of scientific English.

Non-specialised English

Generally, long sentences and big words can be hard to handle. By the time you get to the end of a long sentence, you are likely to have forgotten what was said at the beginning. Big words are often less familiar than the short ones we tend to use in everyday speech. Even when we recognise them, by the time we have pulled their meaning into our consciousness, the talk has moved on and left us behind. At the same time, we often take large steps in our conversation, leaving our listeners to bridge the gaps from their own knowledge. But when that knowledge is shaky, bridging gaps becomes a problem. Add to that some of the grammatical structures we use and an already difficult sentence becomes impenetrable for a novice (for example, 'In the primary distillation process, crude oil is separated into fractions that come off at different temperatures because they have different boiling points'). The rule is: Keep it Simple. There are several formulae that indicate the level of difficulty of a piece of text. One of the simplest is the SMOG formula. Count 30 consecutive sentences. Count the number of words (N) with three or more syllables in these sentences. The year group for which the text is suitable for *unsupported* use is about $3 + \sqrt{N}$ (Newton, 1990). This can help you put books in order of reading ease.

Scientific English

Now add to the above the language of science. Science has words we generally do not use in everyday language. Many of these are polysyllabic words of Graeco-Latin origin that would be transparent to someone with a classical education (for example: anion, bimetal, defecation, endoplasm, herbaceous, lachrymal glands, meniscus, metamorphosis, non-aqueous solvent, olfactory organ, photosynthesis, rectilinear motion, thermal conduction). Others are used in everyday speech but can mean something different in science (for example: cycle, energy, filament, field, incident, material, neutralise, power, selection (as in natural selection), suspension). Still others have passed out of use in everyday speech but remain fossilised in science (for example, *charge* a capacitor, like charging a glass with wine; *vessel* (container), as in blood vessel), and others derive from people's names (such as, galvanometer)). There are grammatical structures like, 'An object on an inclined plane was released so it accelerated down the incline' ('When I let go of the ball-bearing, it went faster and faster down the slope') and 'It is generally believed that' ('I think'). Then there is the effect of mathematics. When this is present, scientific English can be much more difficult to grasp than the SMOG formula suggests (Newton and Merrell, 1994). A quick and easy way of assessing the suitability of a book for a group of pupils is to spread your hand on a page and ask if they understand the words, signs or symbols at your fingertips. If they do not, pupils probably need your support in using the book. When you explain or describe things for pupils, look for body language that tells you that you are talking over their heads. When that happens, backtrack, fill in gaps, and say things in different ways, perhaps using an analogy.

Task 3.8   Making a text message more meaningful

Here are three textbook definitions.

- A species is a group of interbreeding individuals that produce young that can eventually interbreed similarly.
- Energy is the capacity to do work.
- Electrolysis is when chemical change is brought about by a flow of electrical current in a liquid.

Re-write them so they are easier to understand. Your version can be much longer. You may find it helpful to work with colleagues who have specialised in different branches of science. It is worth keeping your elaborations of these definitions for future use.

Learning science is more than learning its laws and explanations in everyday words; it is about becoming comfortable with thinking and communicating using scientific language. You will find that pupils grasp the way you describe things but may not understand the same things in examination papers. Your pupils will eventually have to come to grips with scientific language. While you must be considerate, you need to move the pupils' use of scientific language on gently but firmly. Typically, this is done through scaffolding. When you introduce a concept, you describe it in straightforward, meaningful terms so that the pupils grasp the concept and are not lost in the Forest of Strange Words. Later, you deliberately introduce scientific terms they need to use and pair them with the more familiar, if approximate, terms. Later still, you drop the prop. For example, when you introduce the way a prism disperses white light with younger pupils, you might refer to it as 'spreading out the lamp's light'. Later in the lesson, you might say, 'spreading out the lamp's light or *dispersing* the light'. After you mention that sunlight and lamplight produce more or less 'white light', you may begin to talk of 'spreading out the light or dispersing white light'. At the beginning of the next lesson, you could ask the pupils what 'dispersing white light' means.

Task 3.9   Making words user friendly

Try expressing the following in user-friendly ways for Key Stage 3 pupils.

antagonistic muscles:
habitat:
lifecycle:
photosynthesis:

the states of matter:
saturated solution:
solvent:
a reactivity series:

Task 3.9 *continued*

magnetic field:
moments:
reflection at a plane surface:
amplitude:

Try this task in a tutor group and add the responses to your collection of useful ideas.

Conversations in science

Talking about the science provides useful opportunities to develop your pupils' grasp of scientific language. Sometimes, the demands of a lesson can sideline scientific talk so make opportunities for your pupils to practise using this language. One way is to have an artefact handy to illustrate the point of your lesson and stimulate discussion. I have used an old army pith helmet in this way in work on heat transfer. The outside was white, the inside was lined with foil and there was provision for air flow up past the brow and out through the top of the hat. The conversation, of course, centred on how it might keep someone cool.

You will recall that pupils find lessons engaging when you show enthusiasm, make the topic interesting and are willing to listen to their ideas. Conversations are good times to show some enthusiasm and liking for your subject (but remember that enthusiasm is best when moderate: a display of unbridled enthusiasm may make you the class fool). Conversations also allow you to discover your pupils' scientific interests and have them talk about them. And, of course, you can introduce items that engage them, like the pith helmet did, and listen with interest to their ideas about it. Inevitably, some pupils wanted to try the hat themselves and this was a source of amusement. Pupils should find a lesson at least satisfying, and some teachers are good at using humour in ways that support learning – but never forget that you are a teacher, not a comedian.

SUMMARY

You need a lesson plan, but making it produce what you want depends a lot on what you say and do in the classroom. Your pupils needs to learn facts and figures, see patterns and understand why things are as they are. Do not assume that talking loud and clear or letting pupils experience things for themselves is, in itself, enough. Reduce the mental burden to what is manageable. This can involve breaking a topic into a series of steps that act as a bridge between what your pupils know and what you want them to know. Analogies can help, too, provided you use them with care. However, through all this is the need to get the words right, both yours and the pupils'. Scientific language can add to the difficulties of comprehension but it cannot be sidelined altogether. Think about how to give your pupils a meaningful apprenticeship in its use. Plan as much of such matters as you can beforehand but be prepared for some smart mental footwork in a lesson to keep your pupils thinking productively when they respond in unexpected ways.

Task 3.10 A problem to solve: good plan, shame about the lesson

Dawn had a class of younger, Key Stage 3 pupils. These pupils spanned a relatively wide range of abilities and could be difficult to manage, especially when given practical activities. The scheme of work required Dawn to teach them about mixtures and compounds (to lead in due course to teaching how substances combine).
Her agenda for the lesson was:

1   Ask what the words 'mixture' and 'compound' mean.
2   Demonstrate a mixture of iron filings and powdered sulphur and the making of iron sulphide.
3   Introduce the term 'chemical reaction'.
4   Have the pupils compare mixtures and compounds in a pen-and-paper task.

Some pupils' responses to each item of the agenda are illustrated below. Dawn's reactions to these are included. (P = pupil, T = teacher)

Agenda item 1

T: 'Can anyone tell me what a mixture is?'
P: 'A mixture's a sort of mix, like liquorice allsorts.'
T: 'That's good. Now what about a compound?'
P: [After a long pause] 'Is a compound where you keep prisoners, Miss?'
T: 'Yes, but not in chemistry. Does anyone know? Let's leave it for a minute and have a look at these.'

Agenda item 2:

T: 'This is a pile of iron filings, little bits of iron. Can you all see? This is a pile of powdered sulphur. Are they mixtures?' [Long silence.] 'They are now!' [Dawn mixes some of the iron and sulphur.] 'Do you think we could get the iron and sulphur back again?'
P: [Doubtfully] 'Pick it out . . . with tweezers.'
T: 'How about this. Let's try a magnet.' [Dawn extracts some iron filings.] 'Now watch this!' [Dawn heats some iron and sulphur in a tube with appropriate safety precautions and shows that, once started, a reaction continues and produces a black cinder.] 'Look at this, is it like the mixture we started with?'
P: 'Yes, miss.'
T: 'Do you really think so? [Disappointed.] Look, it's hard and crunchy.'
P: 'It's just that stuff, miss,' [indicating the mixture] 'but you've cooked it. It's like toast.'
T: 'Oh, err, yes, but, err, can I get the iron out again, like we could with the mixture?'
P: 'You'd have to try hard. Oh, look, there's a bit.'
T: [Tries a magnet and the 'bit' sticks to it.] 'Oh, that's a bit that didn't react.'
P: 'Has it gone wrong, miss?'
T: 'No. Everyone watch. I'll crunch the cinder up, like this. See, nothing comes out of it onto the magnet. We've made something different. The iron and sulphur have joined together and we can't get them back. It was just iron and sulphur before. Now it's called iron sulphide. Iron sulphide's nothing like iron or

Task 3.10 *continued*

sulphur. It won't stick to a magnet. Do you all get that?' [Pupils' body language indicates doubt.] 'OK, back to your places.'

Agenda item 3

T: 'What you've just seen happen is called a chemical reaction. Iron is a chemical, sulphur is a chemical, they react together to make a new chemical called iron sulphide. The new chemical is not like the ones we started with.'

Agenda item 4

T: 'OK, settle down. Fold the page to divide it down the middle. [Pause] At the top of the first column, put "Mixtures". At the top of the other column, put "Compounds". Have you all done that? OK, what I want you to do is write as many things as you can about mixtures in the first column and as many things as you can about compounds in the second column.' [Dawn tidies the bench as she knows another teacher is using the room immediately after she leaves it.]

P: [He carefully writes, 'Light black' in the first column. He goes to the second column and neatly writes, 'Dark black'.]

The agenda had promise but the lesson did not go as planned. How would your lesson be different? What would you have said or asked or done to bridge from the known to the unknown? Could a simple analogy have helped? Could item 4 have supported thinking and learning better? Where and how would you do things differently?

You could do this independently or as a group or with the guidance of a tutor.

Afer you have solved the problem, and for those who want a little help, there are some brief notes on page 94.

FURTHER READING

Amos, S. and Boohan, R. (eds) (2002) *Aspects of Teaching Secondary Science*, London: RoutledgeFalmer. 'Talking about science' offers additional advice on questioning, discussing and explaining (5–52).

Frost, J. and Turner, T. (eds) (2005) *Learning to Teach Science in the Secondary School: a companion to school experience*, Abingdon: RoutledgeFalmer. Frost discusses scientific language (178–90) and Sorenson offers further advice on teaching strategies and organising learning (141–56).

Wellington, J. and Osborne, J. (2001) *Language and Literacy in Science Education*, Buckingham: Open University Press. This readable, useful book describes talk, discussion, reading and writing in science education.

Chapter 4   Monitoring and assessing learning in science

Stress at exam time scrambles people's brains.

Harriet Swain

INTRODUCTION

An assessment is what you do when you collect information about your pupils' learning and thinking. It is an important part of teaching, so this chapter is to help you assess thoughtfully and effectively. When assessment comes to mind, thoughts turn to tests and examinations but you can assess in a variety of ways and for a variety of purposes. By the end of the chapter, you should:

- know why assessment is a valuable tool;
- know how you can assess facts, understanding and aspects of practical abilities;
- be aware of some effects of assessment; and
- be aware of the value of simple but effective record keeping.

WHY ASSESS?

There are generally two broad reasons for assessing pupils. The first is to see how their learning and thinking is developing so that you can help them learn and think better. This kind of assessment tends to occur throughout a course and can be informal (as when you ask questions as you teach) or fairly formal (as when you set a short test). You could use what you learn about the pupils to give them feedback and guidance on how to improve, also known as formative assessment. Formative assessment can make a real difference if handled well. You could also use the assessment to diagnose why particular pupils continue to fail on a task. This is less common as it calls for very carefully shaped questions that reveal faulty thinking. Something else that assessments can do is produce better learning directly. When pupils prepare for tests you would expect this but even a quick test at the end of a lesson can help pupils learn as they recall the various elements of the lesson and relate them (Harrison, 2005). Finally, assessment can motivate pupils. For instance, if you teach pupils who believe they usually fail, try giving them a short test before a topic and repeating it afterwards. I speak from experience when I say they often find it very motivating when they see the difference, particularly if they keep a record in the back of their workbooks.

Another reason for assessing pupils is to get a picture of how much they know and can do in order to report it to others. This generally means that the assessment takes place at the end of a course or teaching unit and is called summative assessment. A summative assessment may be a school test you set or it could be a public examination. By their nature, public examinations expose the work of your school to the world (Turner, 2005b). The reputation of the school can rest on the results so they form an important part of head-teachers' thinking. They are, without doubt, important for the school and for the pupils. You should prepare pupils well for such examinations but this does not mean you must continually force feed pupils on facts and figures that they rehearse regularly until they can recite them perfectly. Most school examinations today also give credit for some understanding. Table 4.1 lists various kinds of assessment and what they are used for.

Table 4.1 Various forms of assessment and what they may tell you

Teacher–pupil dialogue	Your discussion and questioning will tell you something about how effective a lesson was. Over a period of time, it can also tell you about pupils' progress. It allows you to provide immediate feedback and has the potential to be powerfully *formative* (Wellington, 1998). Be prepared to adjust your judgements if you follow this with a test.
Class work	Your observation of pupils engaged in a practical activity can add to your views about a pupil's progress. Some work will be written and may add something when you mark it. This can be *formative* in nature.
Homework	Homework may help you assess the effect of your lessons and the pupils' progress, *provided that you set tasks that give you useful information and you mark it with that in mind*. If you then provide constructive feedback, the assessment can be *formative*. Homework that amounts to finishing off classwork, such as the completion of notes, marked more or less for neatness, is less informative (Hayes, 1998).
Self-assessment	Allowing the pupils to comment on the strengths and weaknesses in their learning is becoming more popular. In theory, it has the potential to help pupils take responsibility for their learning. Although pupils are not always able to make sound judgements and act on them, the practice could be valuable if it helps pupils take responsibility for some learning and safe practices. Self- assessment could be *formative* in nature (Bennett, 2003).
Tests	Tests, *if they reflect your objectives*, can provide very useful information regarding your teaching and the pupils' progress. For *formative* purposes, they can focus on relatively small areas of a programme of study, even at the lesson level. For *summative* purposes, the questions generally sample the range of topics covered. Sampling, of course, may not catch what pupils know so you may be unaware of areas of progress simply because you did not ask about them.
Public examinations	Public examinations are generally used as *summative* assessments. Again, they generally test a sample of what has been taught so may miss what a pupil knows and can do. While tests are generally written by you and use words familiar to your pupils, the language of public examinations may seem quite alien to them and they may fail to perform well even on topics they 'know' (Cuthbertson and Frost, 2005).

Task 4.1 Subliminal messages

Your questions, tests, examinations and feedback tell the pupils what counts as worthwhile learning. What message about what counts as important can be inferred from each of the following questions?

Task 4.1 *continued*

1   Draw and label the parts of a typical plant cell.
2   Name three allotropes of carbon.
3   State the formula that relates force, mass and acceleration.
4   Calculate the current through the bulb when there are 3 volts across it and the bulb's resistance is 6 ohms.
5   Balance the following chemical equation.
6   A wooden plank is found to balance on bricks so that 2m is on one side and 1m is on the other. What does this tell you about the plank?
7   A gene relating to sight is found on the X chromosome. In normal sight, it is dominant. In colour blindness, it is recessive. Draw a diagram to work out the consequences for the male and female children of a father with normal sight and a mother who is colour blind.
8   Suppose someone was painted all over so that every bit of skin was covered with a waterproof paint. What effect could this have on the person's health?
9   Bars of zinc are attached to the sides of steel ships to prevent rusting. Why does this work?
10 The advertisements say that a new catalyst called 'Velochem' works well in catalytic converters on cars. It claims it makes more carbon monoxide and bad hydrocarbons harmless than existing catalysts. A scientist is given the task of testing it. He takes two identical cars and fits one with a conventional converter and one with a Velochem converter. Both cars are side by side and contain the same kind of petrol. He warms up both engines for the same length of time and tests the exhaust gases. He finds little difference between them. Has he done enough to say that Velochem is no better than existing catalytic converters? Explain your answer.

Some of the different types of questions are discussed later.

Task 4.2   What constructive, formative feedback would you provide?

Younger pupils did a practical activity that involved a strip of wood supported in the middle. They placed two masses at different positions on one side and balanced them with one mass on the other side. The intention was that the pupils would see the pattern in the data they collected. This is the account of one pupil.

Results

Left-hand side Distance to middle		Right-hand side Distance to middle
100 g mass	200 g mass	300 g mass
15 cm	10 cm	12 cm
10 cm	5 cm	7 cm
10 cm	20 cm	17 cm

Conclusion

What we found was we always had to put the 300g so that it was halfway between the other numbers. Then it balanced. It wasn't exact but it is near enough. This is because of experimental errors. You just have to add the first two numbers and halve the answer to get the other one.

First, provide written, constructive, formative feedback.

Second, discuss with colleagues or your tutor what you could do in the next lesson to address the problem.

ASSESSING FACTUAL KNOWLEDGE

This is about assessing a pupil's possession of factual information (or, more precisely, his or her ability to recall it on demand). The obvious way to do this is to ask for the information you seek. So, for instance, you might ask:

What do we call the vessels that carry blood away from the heart?
What is the symbol for sodium?
What does mA mean?

At times, you may want to see if pupils can recall a sentence you told them. For example:

What is the purpose of the skin?
What is a noble gas?
What are the laws of reflection?

Of course, just because the pupils can tell you what you want to hear does not mean they understand the purpose of the skin, the nature of a noble gas, or the laws of reflection. Nevertheless, if recall of facts and statements is important, you must ask for it. There are various ways of testing for factual knowledge. Suppose you asked for the equation that links force, mass and acceleration; you might use a multiple choice format in which the pupil selects an answer:

(a) $F = m/a$
(b) $F = a/m$
(c) $F = ma$
(d) $F = mga$
(e) $F = mv$

Such questions are easy to mark but they often call for recognition rather than recall, and recognition can be easier than recall. They can be made more demanding in the following way:

The purpose of the skin is to:

I Signal touch.
II Make vitamin C.
III Store fat.
IV Prevent other body parts becoming dry.
V Store protein.

Answer

(a) if you think I, II, III, IV are correct.
(b) if you think I, IV, V are correct.
(c) if you think I, III, IV, V are correct.
(d) if you think I, III, IV are correct.
(e) if you think II, IV, V are correct.

Finding convincing alternatives for such questions can be difficult and some pupils may guess and have a lucky day. Guessing effects, however, become less of a problem as the test length increases. To sum up, there are various ways of checking on factual knowledge and these include:

• short answer questions;
• multiple choice questions;
• drawing a diagram;
• labelling a diagram;
• supplying missing words in sentences (with or without a word bank);
• pairing related items (e.g. by drawing a line between a diagram and a word).

Task 4.3 'Now, what I want is Facts,' said Mr Gradgrind (*Hard Times* by Charles Dickens).

Construct questions that test factual knowledge in three different ways and relate to one of the topics: ecosystems, fossil fuels or water pressure (or to a topic you will soon teach).

Question 1

Question 2

Question 3

Try them out on your colleagues (or on pupils).

ASSESSING UNDERSTANDING AND PRODUCTIVE THINKING

Understanding is about seeing connections between things. To test for it, ask yourself what pupils should be able to *do* if they understand. Once that is clear, you ask them to do it. Understanding in science gives a pupil the ability to:

- explain in his or her own words, tell you why, provide reasons and justify actions and assertions;
- think flexibly, solve new problems and apply what they know in new situations;
- make predictions;
- think critically and evaluate evidence.

To illustrate, here are some examples.

Explaining

These questions relate to work that may have been discussed in the classroom but the explanations must be expressed in the pupils' own words.

> Explain the cause of thunder.
> You sometimes see small tunnels under roads for hedgehogs. Why are they good for an ecosystem?
> Tell me, in your own words, why heating the mixture is a good idea?

Flexible thinking

These questions would not have been discussed in class.

> Dried peas, frozen chips and heat-treated milk last longer than untreated peas, chips and milk. For each one, explain why.
> When bubbles that start at the bottom of a glass of lemonade rise to the surface, they become bigger. Why?

Predicting

Again, these questions would not have been answered prior to the test.

> What would happen if all the plants in the world died? Why?
> What would happen if you added twice as much salt? Would it all dissolve? Why do you think that?
> Do you think this will conduct electricity? Why do you think that?

Thinking critically

> I suspect that all insects like to hide in dark places, under stones and in rubbish. Here is an experiment to test that idea. A bottle has some small beetles (that normally live on flowers) rushing around in it. The bottle is now placed in the shade. The beetles stop rushing around. I think this is evidence that they like dark places because they are calmer there. What do you think? Why?

Generally, questions about understanding take more time to answer than factual questions. They also often take more time to mark. Sometimes, hard-pressed teachers avoid them in favour of factual questions. A consequence is that the pupils learn that understanding and 'higher' level thought do not matter and that science is about learning facts. Even as adults, many people continue to believe this. So, you really do need to include 'thinking' questions in your tests and examinations if you want your pupils to value thought and understanding in science and to become better at it. It is possible to make some questions easy to mark. Here is an example (note, however, it still allows guessing).

What makes a solid bar of iron sink in a dish of water?

(a) The dish is not deep enough.
(b) There is not enough water to float the iron bar.
(c) The iron gets wet.
(d) The weight of a bar of iron is greater than the weight of water it pushes aside.
(e) The bar must not have the ends curved up so that they are out of the water.

To sum up, here are some kinds of question that you might try asking in assessing for understanding and application:

- questions with a space for an explanation of two or three sentences;
- questions that ask for an extended explanation of a paragraph or more, perhaps supported by a diagram;
- multiple choice questions, which provide alternative explanations to choose from;
- questions that ask for predictions;
- questions asking for a justification of a course of action, prediction or conclusion;
- asking pupils to think of another example of a phenomenon or event and justify their choice;
- problems of various kinds to solve, varying in the extent to which they match the examples you used in class;
- presented explanations and investigations to criticise, identifying their strengths and weaknesses.

Task 4.4 Questions of understanding

Construct three different kinds of question to test a pupil's understanding of central aspects of one of the topics: ecosystems, fossil fuels or water pressure (or a topic you will soon teach). If at all possible, work on the same topic as in Task 4.3. It may help to keep in mind the key question: Why? Make at least one question relatively easy to mark.

Question 1

Question 2

Question 3

Try them out on your colleagues (or on pupils).

ASSESSING INVESTIGATIVE ABILITIES

The problem with assessing investigative abilities is that they are complex beasts and it takes time. Investigations can include:

- grasping the nature of the problem (finding out what it means and what is involved);
- planning (beginning with a prediction then designing an experiment to test it, controlling variables, deciding the kind and amount of data to collect, choosing techniques and equipment);
- collecting, organising and presenting information (using equipment and materials appropriately and safely, measuring to a suitable degree of precision, organising data and presenting them effectively);
- weighing evidence (considering the data's quality, looking for patterns and relationships, drawing relevant conclusions, explaining and justifying the conclusions);
- evaluating (noting data that do not fit the pattern and seeking reasons for them, considering the need for further investigation, thinking of ways in which the investigation might be improved).

Scientific problems may not provide opportunities to demonstrate each of these equally. At the same time, you would find trying to assess everything for everyone in the class with one investigation quite demanding. It can be easier to build a picture of practical ability as pupils work over several investigations. Where do these investigations come from?

Ideally, problems to investigate would arise as you introduce and develop a topic. So, for instance, if you were doing work on seed dispersal and showed sycamore seeds, the pupils may draw your attention to joined pairs of seeds that look like aeroplanes and to single-winged, single-seed forms. You could ask: Are the latter simply accidents? Which is best for the tree, a whirling, single-winged form or a gliding, double-winged seed? Can they find out? Using interests and ideas in this way can be very motivating for pupils. A difficulty is that their ideas can be unpredictable and you may not have the equipment or have a relevant risk assessment. At the same time, even the best class may not come up with a problem when you need it. This means that teachers tend to have ideas for investigations ready. Often, these are included in the scheme of work along with a risk assessment. What is lost in spontaneity may be gained, to some extent, in efficiency.

Task 4.5   You think you've got a problem?

For one of the following topics, think of a problem that could lead to a prediction, and a practical investigation that could engage pupils' interest. Anticipate various ways your pupils might test the prediction. Can they be attempted safely? If necessary, consult your tutor for advice.

Choose from:

- a healthy diet;
- the corrosion of metals;
- friction.

If you give the pupils an investigation you should assess their responses. Look again at the list of investigative skills above. How, for instance, do you assess planning, collecting information or weighing evidence? It is obviously not enough simply to check each on a Yes/No basis. Nor is it particularly useful to ask: Is the planning good? Is the weighing of evidence better than last time? What constitutes 'good' and 'better'? Often, a science department has marking schemes that state behaviours that count as good, fair and weak in each of these areas. If not, consult Attainment Target 1 in the National Curriculum Order for Science, where some attempt has been made to rank levels of skill (www.nc.uk.net).

For example, at Level 3, your pupils can carry out a fair test with some help and can tell you what makes it fair. They can notice simple patterns in their data and point to ways of improving their investigation. At Level 4, they can decide on the approach so that they vary one factor and control the others. They can make predictions themselves, identify patterns using graphs and begin to relate their conclusions to these patterns. At Levels 5 and 6, levels expected of most pupils in Key Stage 3, they identify an approach and key factors to consider, make predictions using their scientific knowledge and understanding, and their conclusions are consistent with the evidence. This sounds very useful but, in practice, it can be difficult to assign a level because it all depends on your interpretation of the descriptors. What, for instance, is a 'simple' pattern? What is the difference between relating conclusions to patterns in the data and drawing conclusions that are consistent with the evidence?

Suppose at some point you have to decide what counts as Level 3, 4 or 5 for a particular activity. This is much easier if you work as a team and agree specific differences in performance you will look for. If this way of working is not possible, then try the following:

- put the pupils' work in order from 'best' investigation to 'worst' investigation, using an overall judgement;
- if this is at the end of Key Stage 3, most of your pupils should be in the Level 5/6 band so choose two or three from the middle and compare them with the descriptors for those levels; if they match, assign that level; if not, look at the levels on either side;
- now look at the best work and the descriptors above the level you have just assigned until you find a match;
- do the same with the worst work, comparing them with the levels below what you assigned to the middle group;
- check borderline work and adjust the level awarded if there is good reason to do so;
- some schools have examples of work to illustrate each level of attainment and, if these are available, compare your pupils' work with these;
- have a colleague give an opinion on your 'levelling' without, of course, expecting your colleague to spend as much time as you on it (and do the same for him or her).

It could take several investigations before you begin to feel some confidence in the grade or level awarded. Roberts and Gott (2004), however, have proposed the use of written evidence tests to assess 'the thinking behind the doing'. Such a question could be:

Golden and Bounty are popular turnip seeds but they suffer from pests. Scientists produced two new varieties called Golden GM and Bounty GM. They thought these would be pest-resistant and produce bigger crops.

A farmer is asked to try all four kinds of seed. He has five fields available: two with clay soil, two with a sand/clay mix soil, and one with sandy soil. All five fields are flat and receive the same sunlight and rain.

(a) How would you test the seeds to see if the new breeds are better than the old breeds? (You can use any, some or all of these fields.) This is what the farmer actually did:

Field	Seed planted	Weight harvested (tonnes)
Clay	Golden	3.7
Clay	Golden GM	4.1
Clay/sand	Bounty	4.3
Clay/sand	Golden GM	4.6
Sandy	Bounty GM	3.1

The farmer concluded that:

1 Golden GM seed is more productive than Golden.
2 Golden GM seed is more productive than Bounty GM seed.
3 Bounty seed is more productive than Bounty GM.
4 Golden GM seed is more productive than Bounty.

(b) Which of these is a sound conclusion?
(c) Which of these is unsound?
(d) Is there evidence that the soil makes a difference? Explain your answer.

Task 4.6 Assessing the thinking behind the doing

Construct a pencil and paper test to assess some aspect of investigating for the practical problem you thought of in Task 4.5.
   If possible, try it out on some pupils or ask for your tutor's opinion of it.

Task 4.7 Using case studies

There are several ways of assessing a pupil's grasp of the scientific process and the way scientists work. So that your pupils find the topic meaningful, you could invent a tale of weak science and ask pupils to find the faults. On the other hand, you might ask the pupils to discuss real issues, such as the causes and effects of global warming. The problem is that such debates are very complex but, provided you keep it simple rather than simplistic, it could be worthwhile. Here is an example.

There was a time when most doctors believed that living things could develop from dead materials. So, for instance, maggots developed in and from meat. Nevertheless, Francesco Redi, an Italian doctor, believed maggots developed

Task 4.7 continued

from eggs laid by flies. To test his belief, he put pieces of meat in jars. Some jars were sealed and others were open to the air. Only the meat open to the air developed maggots.

Redi felt he had made his point but other doctors said that all he had shown was that maggots needed air to develop from meat. Redi did another experiment. He put meat in jars and covered the jars with gauze cloth. Even though the air could get through the cloth, no maggots developed.

People were still reluctant to give up the idea of life developing out of dead materials and, when microscopes were invented, they saw small living things on just about everything. For instance, if a piece of hay fell in water and was left for a few days, small, living things grew on it. They pointed to this as evidence that they were right.

The French chemist, Louis Pasteur, was interested in what makes food go off and how to prevent it happening. He had two kinds of glass flasks. The neck of one flask pointed up in the normal way but the other had a curved neck that pointed down so things in the air could not fall in. Pasteur put some broth in both and boiled it to kill anything in it. He then left the flasks for several days. The broth in the normal flask went off very quickly but the broth in the other flask stayed fresh.

Some doctors still held their belief that living things grow out of dead things. Other scientists tried to convince them they were wrong. For instance, John Tyndall made a sealed box with a glass front. When he shone a strong light through it, he could see bits floating in the air. Under the microscope, these bits had tiny, living things on them so he filtered the air until it was clear. He found that food that had been heated stayed fresh much longer in boxes of filtered air.

Of course, doctors today know that there are microbes in the air and some of these make food go off and cause illnesses. Living things were not growing from dead things. What they saw were the effects of life in the microscopic world.

Plan how you would use this case study and list the questions you would ask.

Discuss your plan and questions with your tutor and, if possible, try them out on some pupils.

ACTIVE ASSESSMENT

Formal testing can get in the way of doing and learning science. Moreover, some pupils never do well in examinations because nerves get the better of them. *Active assessment* is a part of a normal lesson. For example, you might give pupils a worksheet describing 'a scientist's experiment' with procedural errors in it for them to spot. Another worksheet might ask pupils to list up to three things about electricity they know well, up to three they are not sure about, and up to three they need to know better. Still another might be to sort cards with statements about energy into piles of, 'I agree', 'I do not agree', and, 'It depends'. As a group activity, it can tell you about the success of your lesson. Done by individuals, it can tell you about your lesson and that person's learning. Here is a short list of some things you might do (Naylor *et al.*, 2004):

- For things that change over time, give the pupils a cartoon strip with the first picture done for them. They complete the rest to show the progression over time.
- To see how well pupils relate concepts (e.g. voltage, power, resistance), give them a set of cards with the concepts written on them and a set of 'joining' words (e.g. 'depends on', 'is the same'). They arrange and relate the concepts.
- To gauge pupils' thinking about a topic, have them think of parallels with an analogy (e.g. a leaf is like a factory because . . .).
- To judge how well pupils grasp concepts, have them find the odd one out and explain why they chose that one (e.g. rusting, burning, melting).

Task 4.8   Trying to keep active

Construct an active assessment task to use in a part of your lesson on:

- inheritance; *or*
- symbol equations in chemistry; *or*
- the electromagnetic spectrum.

(If necessary, add to your knowledge of active assessment using the Internet.)

Try the task out on a class.

REPORTING ON PROGRESS IN LEARNING

Reporting to parents, guardians and carers

You have to report internal summative assessments to whoever has responsibility for the pupil. Each school usually has a reporting system you must follow. This system tells you some of the information you must include in the report, such as the mark or grade showing the level of achievement and, perhaps, some indication of how this compares with the other pupils. You may also have to provide a grade indicating the effort made by the pupil (although comments about effort tend to reflect examination marks). By themselves, figures and grades may not convey a lot so it is usual to add a comment. Because you are used to the language, abbreviations and euphemisms of school life they may slip into your comments and can be obscure to a non-teacher. Make your comments clear and concise, and do not patronise. Tell parents what your professional judgement is about their child's progress in learning and, if there is a notable strength, you could mention it. A serious weakness, such as not doing homework or preparing for tests, may also have to be brought to parents' attention as they need to be made aware, and may be able to help address it. Always bear in mind that you may not have the full story: pupils have lives outside school.

Usually, you also have face-to-face meetings with parents or carers to report on a pupil's progress. Prepare by making a few notes on a class list. For instance, note how the performance has changed since last time, how the pupil responds in class and, if appropriate, any evidence of aptitude in science. Again, avoid jargon. Have to hand a note of what you wrote on the report – you would look foolish if you could not recall it or, worse, confused it with what you wrote about someone else. You could have with you a piece of good work done by the pupil. It can be an ice-breaker and ease the way should there be less happy things to discuss: 'So, this is what I know she can do. Unfortunately . . .'. When there are things to address, have examples to hand to show parents or carers. This makes the point clearer. You may feel that setting specific targets for a pupil could help. It can be difficult for parents to know what they can do; after all, you are the teacher. Tactfully, see if you can enlist parents' or carers' support: 'I'm a little concerned – I imagine you are, too.' With some pupils, you may also have to advise about course options. Options can have long-term consequences so your advice should be professional, considered and informative. Whatever you do, do not discuss other pupils or make comparisons with particular individuals.

Task 4.9 Who's a clever boy/girl, then?

This is what one science teacher wrote on a pupil's report at the end of the term: 'Promises to try harder next term'. At the end of the next term, he wrote, 'So much for promises.'

Comments like these are understandable. Frustration, exasperation and defeat bring out the teaching equivalent of graveyard humour. You, however, are made of sterner stuff. Discuss with your colleagues or your tutor what could be a more constructive comment.

Reporting to others

Assessments are used to monitor a school's performance. Schools vary in location and intake, something referred to as the 'context'. Schools could, therefore, check their performance by comparing themselves with similar schools. Alternatively, a school may measure the 'value' it adds to pupils' learning by comparing pupils' performance when they arrive with what it is when they leave. You may need to supply information so that your school can gauge its performance each year. Data from Standard Assessment Tests (SATs) and General Certificate for Secondary Education (GCSE) grades are also processed by the DfES (Department for Education and Skills) to produce 'benchmarks' against which schools compare themselves. One benchmark is the proportion of pupils gaining A* to C grades in GCSE science, and this is directly relevant to your work. Note that benchmarks can change from year to year as examination results change. Information like this is available to the public through performance tables and a school's position in them matters. Schools generally strive to improve their position and may have strategies in place to support that (Turner, 2005b; Hayes, 1998).

SUMMARY

Assessment has several purposes, loosely divided into assessment for learning and assessment of learning. The former uses the results to guide and support further learning (formative assessment). The latter uses them to gauge the quality and quantity of learning of a pupil at a given point in time (summative assessment). Formative assessment is generally an ongoing process that helps you provide useful feedback. If this is thoughtful and constructive, it can support further learning. Summative assessment produces information to report to parents, carers and others. You can assess different kinds of thinking and learning, typically memorisation, understanding and application. There are various ways you could test each of these. The danger is that pressure of time leads you to focus on learning that is easy to assess, such as memorisation. Pupils then believe this is what science is about. Assessing practical skills can be time-consuming and difficult. Consider time-saving approaches that assess the thinking that underpins an investigation but do not make them a substitute for hands-on activity in your day-to-day teaching. Reporting to parents and carers needs to be informative but considerate. Other data collected by you may contribute to judgements of a school's performance.

Task 4.10   A problem to solve: a matter of taste

The end of term, one-hour examination is approaching for your Year 8, mixed ability science class. The topics this term were:

- principles of human digestion, the role of acid and enzymes, absorption of nutrients and transport in the bloodstream, waste product egestion;
- acids and bases, classifying solutions using indicators, acid corrosion of metals, rock weathering, acid rain, indigestion, everyday applications of neutralisation;
- energy sources, including food, the Sun as a primary source of energy, renewable and non-renewable sources.

Although this is how the topics were listed in the scheme of work, you taught them in a way that highlighted connections between them and included various kinds of practical activity, including investigations. During the investigations, you were a little surprised to find that some pupils drew 'conclusions' that did not relate directly to the question asked so you spent time on that.

Task 4.10 *continued*

The examination should reveal knowledge and understanding. Construct a set of questions centred upon one of these topics that most of the pupils could attempt in about 20 minutes.

If you can, collate your questions with those of colleagues who centred their questions on the other topics. Do they sit comfortably together? What gives rise to any unevenness? Would they be better if they were edited by one person?

After you have solved the problem, and for those who want a little help, there are some brief notes on page 94.

FURTHER READING

Daws, N. and Singh, B. (1999) 'Formative assessment strategies in secondary school science', *School Science Review*, 80(293): 71–8. This is a useful article which describes specific strategies for assessing science.

Dobson, J. (2005) 'Assessing and monitoring progress in secondary science', in L.D. Newton (ed.) *Meeting the Standards in Secondary Science*, London: Routledge: 207–19. This chapter offers a clear account of the purposes and practice of assessment.

Frost. J. and T. Turner (eds), *Learning to Teach Science in the Secondary School: a companion to school experience*, 2nd edn, Abingdon: RoutledgeFalmer. See especially Cuthbertson and Frost on public examinations (225–40), Harrison on assessing for learning (211–24), and Turner on accountability and reporting (241–48).

Naylor, S., Keogh, B. and Goldsworthy, A. (2004) *Active Assessment*, London: Fulton. This is a very readable book with practical examples of active assessment.

QCA (Qualifications and Curriculum Authority) (2005) *Assessing Progress in Science*, London: QCA. You may find these useful teacher development materials (guide, booklets and CD-ROM) in school or in your training institution.

Chapter 5   Differences

Every child matters.

Title of a series of DfES publications

INTRODUCTION

Pupils are different. They think and learn in different ways and with various degrees of success, they see the world differently and have different values, and some may have to interact with the world in different ways. You must do your best for all of them. As examples, this chapter describes different ways of learning, successful and unsuccessful learners, some gender effects, cultural differences, and disability and access to learning. It illustrates how you might do your best in such contexts. By the end of this chapter you will:

- know some common ways in which pupils are different;
- know how to help particular pupils achieve more.

WAYS OF LEARNING

We all have preferred ways of working and this is probably true of the way we learn. Some say they prefer to listen and learn while others claim they learn more by doing it for themselves. Some seem to benefit from a preliminary overview to show how everything fits together while others seem to be happy without one. It could be a good idea to teach in ways that recognise such diversity, but what does this mean in practice? The problem is that people seem to think up learning preferences and styles at the drop of a hat. One popular set, for instance, is the *visual* learner (learning by seeing), the *auditory* learner (learning by hearing) and the *kinaesthetic* learner (learning by doing), known as the VAK model. Some add learners who prefer *text* (reading/writing) to make it the VARK model. Others add pupils who learn by *touch*. Another system lists *sensory, intuitive, visual, verbal, active, reflective, sequential*, and *global* learners (Felder, 1988). Elsewhere are *reflectors, theorists, activists* and *pragmatists* (Honey and Mumford, 1982). Others talk of *field dependence* and *field independence, visualisers* and *verbalisers, holistic* and *analytic* learners (Riding and Raynor, 1999). Then there are *active experimenters, reflective observers, concrete experiencers*, and *abstract conceptualisers* (Kolb, 1984), *innovative, analytic, common sense*, and *dynamic* learners (McCarthy, 1980).

The abundance of lists of learning styles and the weak basis of many of them can make you uncertain of what to do (Coffield *et al.*, 2004). But, if you take a step back from the detail, you see that variety can:

- reduce the risk of pupil boredom and add to your own interest; variety can also improve attitudes to school science (Osborne, 2003);
- provide more opportunities for your pupils to grasp the point: if they did not quite understand your explanation, they have another chance when you put the object in their hands;
- recognise that people may have their own, effective ways of thinking and may learn better in some circumstances than in others.

What could this variety in teaching look like? Information can be presented in several ways. Suppose you have to teach the human circulatory system over the next few lessons. You could begin with a short, interactive overview of learning goals and show why they are important (referring to a picture of blocked arteries). Then you could explain the circulatory system using your own body as a reference point for locating organs and directions of blood flow. Add to that a plastic model of the body for pupils to take apart and match to your words and a stethoscope to listen to the heart. You could then have pupils explain it to you with the help of a wallchart showing the system. Because doing something themselves can reinforce learning, you might have pupils fit together a jigsaw of the system, working in pairs. They could also prepare a cartoon strip by themselves to show a day in the life of a red blood cell, or write an account of it using a textbook. After that, they might investigate the effect of physical activity on their heart rates. To conclude, you could use a short role play activity to show how red blood cells behave. Some pupils may prefer to sit the last one out and observe or provide the explanation.

This approach provides an overall view of the topic for those who benefit from a global structure. You supported visual (pointing to yourself, the model, the chart) and auditory ways of learning (verbal account and stethoscope sounds). By including the pupils in your explanation and through the subsequent activities, you provided for tactile (touch) and kinaesthetic (activity) preferences. You also made some allowance for learning through interaction (paired work and heart rate activity) and individual work, and for those who prefer writing and reading (alternative to the cartoon sequence).

Sometimes, you may be able to focus on a narrower range of approaches. This is more likely when you have classes that are streamed or set by ability but remember that narrowing ability does not always narrow the need for variety. In addition, some pupils may need to develop more effective ways of learning, so focusing only on their preferences may not do them a favour. You may find it useful to think in terms of functional and dysfunctional thinkers and aim to replace ineffective behaviours with those that are more effective (Jackson, 2002).

Task 5.1 Variety is the spice of life

You have to explain the meaning of *pure* as the term is used in science.

All the pupils in your class learn, to some extent, by seeing, hearing and doing. Some are happier watching you do things and then reinforcing and extending it with a book if it is readable, well-illustrated and includes interesting, everyday examples. Others prefer doing things for themselves.

What would be the steps in your lesson?

Task 5.1 *continued*

How would your lesson reflect pupils' learning preferences?

Discuss with your tutor or colleagues the pros and cons of what you propose to do.

THE SUCCESSFUL PUPIL

One or two of your pupils may catch on quickly, seem to learn with ease and generally do well in examinations. You probably describe these as 'able' or 'gifted'. It is easy to see these as not needing much of your time, but they deserve your attention if they are to make the most of the abilities they have.

How do you recognise gifted pupils in science? The easy answer is to point to test results and the quality of everyday work. Pupils to consider are those who also tend to ask 'Why?' This suggests they are not satisfied with descriptions and seek understanding. Those who grasp and use ideas quickly and explore their implications, those who tend to see the whole picture, construct sound experiments, see clearly how data reflects on the question asked and see an experiment's limitations are also likely candidates. Outside school, these pupils may have a strong interest in a science-related hobby but keep it to themselves. Also ask yourself if there are one or two others who are overlooked because their work tends to be untidy or they do not shine in examinations. It is said that Einstein and Darwin did not show early potential. What can you do for gifted pupils? In teacher-speak, you can *enrich*, *extend* or *accelerate* their studies.

Enrichment involves providing things to think about that widen knowledge and skills and help it all hang together as a whole. So, for instance, when doing work on magnetism, you may have these pupils compare and contrast magnetism and static electricity (involving independent study of the latter). Extension, on the other hand, involves going deeper into a subject. In magnetism, you might ask how quickly the force falls off with distance. Can the pupil devise some sort of test to see how it dies away? Finally, acceleration means working through the subject at a faster pace. This is not easy to manage in a mixed ability class without some independent study. In a large school with ability grouping, it becomes feasible and such a class may sometimes be entered early for examinations. Occasionally, a pupil may be promoted to a class of older pupils. This is not always satisfactory because being gifted in science does not imply equal abilities elsewhere and a pupil's social skills may suffer. But the least you should be able to do in any class is tailor your questions to the needs of your pupils, make some tasks more open-ended and challenge them with additional thought about the topic.

Task 5.2 Enrich and extend

Some gifted pupils finish their work early and say nothing. Choose a topic (e.g. adaptation of organisms, solubility, or refraction of light) and develop:

(a) an enrichment idea; and
(b) an extension idea

for more able Key Stage 3 pupils. Plan how to manage this extra dimension of a lesson and, if possible, try out your ideas.

Task 5.3 Personal projects

In Key Stage 4 you can enrich and extend pupils' knowledge through a *personal project*. A personal project can start with a topic you taught in class but a pupil takes it further in a more or less self-directed way. Personal projects can be on quite unusual topics. For example, following a session about parasites, one pupil brought up the subject of insect galls on leaves and how the galls were once used to make ink. Insect galls became his personal project. He made a collection of galls and compiled and organised a box file of notes and materials. The teacher showed interest, asked about progress and took care not to let the project outlive its interest. In the conversations, good thought was praised and ideas were suggested. Sometimes, it may be possible to turn the project into a safe, practical investigation that the pupil may do at home.

Choose two topics from the list below and identify possible personal projects for them. Books that look at the subject broadly may help, or research the topics using the Internet.

Sensing the environment

Air pollution

The Earth

Mendeléev's periodic table

Gravity

Waves

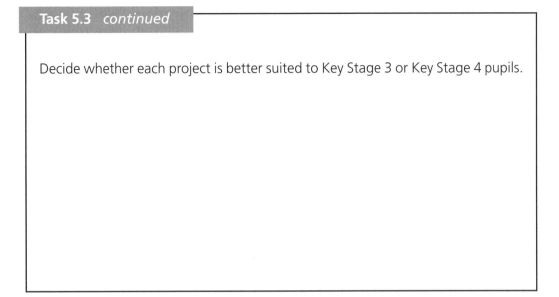

Task 5.3 *continued*

Decide whether each project is better suited to Key Stage 3 or Key Stage 4 pupils.

THE UNSUCCESSFUL PUPIL

This group includes those who struggle in science, show little ability and have difficulty learning. It also includes those who are reluctant to learn. Unsuccessful pupils may attend erratically, arrive without pen, pencil or books, work slowly, pay intermittent and short attention, may lose interest relatively quickly and be easily distracted, tend not to cope with complex tasks and what they learn in one context is not transferred readily to another.

How do you help such pupils? Observe them carefully and try to find out what contributes to their lack of success. Do they recall what they did last week? Do they recall it but do not see its relevance? Does it take a long time for them to make connections? Are the gaps too big for them to cross? Usually, such pupils are unsuccessful for a variety of reasons but you can support them if you know the cause. Sometimes it may be language difficulties for which there could be additional help available (Weatherhead *et al.*, 2004 offer a useful case study). Other pupils may not retain the main message of the lesson. For instance, you had your pupils squeeze water out of a piece of moss to find, with the help of a microscope, that the water contains living things. Your aim was to show that even unprepossessing moss is a place to live for some things. But your pupils remember the organisms, not the more general message. These pupils need *organised thought and action, small steps, varied and frequent practice* and your *support*. Here are some things you might try:

- before a lesson, remove or reduce distractions and plan how to organise and manage things to minimise them;
- keep your lesson structure simple and use it regularly so the pupils come to know it;
- begin by helping pupils recall any prior learning they will need in this lesson;
- break down the topic into small, manageable steps, make sure the pupils can see the connections, ensure they engage with each step through, for instance, discussion, oral questions or an activity, have them respond in different ways to a key idea (they may explain it orally, draw and label it, and think of another example of it). These pupils may not hold concepts or ideas in their minds for long so you need to reinforce each one regularly;
- divide the chalkboard into two parts; use one part as a working space and the other as a tidy note pad to record what they need to know;
- if the work involves reading a textbook or worksheet, preview it orally with the pupils;
- allow time to do work properly; praise completed work that shows effort;
- have pupils practise what they learn in different ways;

- emphasise that success comes through time, effort, persistence, co-operation and help;
- show you care about their learning by interacting and supporting individuals;
- take pleasure in success, even when it is small;
- keep adding to your repertoire of approaches (e.g. Keogh and Naylor, 2002).

Task 5.4 Structure and support

Suppose that you think your less able pupils now understand that a leaf is like a factory for producing sugars which the plant uses for energy and growth. This week's big idea is for them to grasp something else the leaf does, namely, that it is a major player in transpiration. By enabling and controlling water loss, the leaf helps to establish a suitable flow of liquid from the roots through the plant and this brings much needed substances in from the soil. During the lesson, each pupil has a leafy twig in a beaker of water. On the top of the water is a thin layer of cooking oil. Chinograph pencils are available for marking the side of the beaker.

1   Identify matters and parts that may cause difficulty for less able learners.

2   How do you help less able pupils overcome the difficulties?

3   Think of a safe, practical investigation these learners might try with this equipment.

4   What problems, if any, do you anticipate in the investigation and how do you address them?

It may help to share ideas with colleagues or a tutor before you work on the detail yourself.

There are limits to what we can hold in our minds and think about. If the demand is too great, thinking suffers or people simply give up. This can happen in the work you set for pupils. For instance, if an investigation involves drawing a graph, the thought needed to draw the graph may obscure the point of the activity. The patterns in many school science activities hardly need a graph to make them apparent and you could discuss the pattern in data directly. After that, you could use the data to draw a graph on a transparency on an overhead projector, having the pupils take turns to mark on their points.

Task 5.5 Taking the strain

Consider an investigation (one you have taught, one in a school textbook, or one in a scheme of work). An investigation generally involves:

- an aim;
- the design of an experiment;
- the running of the experiment;
- data collection and evaluation;
- data processing;
- drawing a relevant conclusion and knowing its limits.

Thinking of your investigation, where might a less skilful thinker have difficulty? Choose one of the difficulties and consider how you would reduce it. This task can benefit from sharing your thoughts with colleagues or a tutor.

Some pupils have particular conditions that make it difficult for them to learn. Autism, for example, can severely impair interaction skills so that social situations make such pupils very anxious. As with all pupils, the variation from one to another can be large. While those with classic autism can experience severe learning difficulties, those with related conditions may have average or above average intellectual abilities. Such pupils may benefit from a structured, sheltered environment and from specialist help in the classroom. The area of special educational needs encompasses such pupils and is a specialism of some teachers. If you have a chance to observe one at work, you may learn some useful tips about lesson pace, step size and frequent practice.

Reluctant learners, on the other hand, would generally be considered to be your concern. Some have a negative attitude to school and a half-hearted engagement with tasks. Others can be difficult to distinguish from less able pupils because they may share some of their characteristics, such as intermittent attention. They can, however, work relatively quickly in order to dispose of a task. As a consequence, the product is likely to be of low quality and reflect thought avoidance. Having finished, they may now seek to distract others.

If you are satisfied that a pupil has the ability to learn fairly readily but avoids it, you could look to motivational strategies for help (Chapter 3) and try to use pupils' interests. If their reward for not participating comes from the peer group, however, you may need to target the group as a whole. The aim is to have what they do attract them more than the alternatives. One attractive approach is to begin with a part of a television programme suitable for that age group. So, for instance, if you want to do some work on food properties and healthy eating with younger pupils, there is King Size Homer, when Homer Simpson eats himself to vast proportions. Similarly, Wallace and Gromit could provide starting points for work on kinds of energy. For slightly older pupils, Crime Scene Investigation and forensic science programmes can provide ways into topics like blood (always plenty of that) and DNA. Advertisements that compare products like soap may make starting points for investigations. In due course, try weaning your pupils from fiction and advertisements. News items about, for instance, the MRSA Superbug, are also potential sources of interest and programmes about wildlife can lead to work on habitats (see Rodrigues *et al.*, undated). Check that it is permissible to use extracts from a television programme or recording for educational purposes in a school.

Task 5.6 Reluctant learning

Plan how to work with a class in which there are two reluctant learners with several admirers who sometimes copy their behaviour. The topics are:

- functions of the skeleton;
- rocks in the Earth's crust;
- radioactive substances.

How would you catch interest in these?

What materials would you use?

Either alone or with a group of colleagues, generate ideas.

Consult a tutor about the suitability of these ideas.

GENDER

Science has several sides to it and you need to be clear which side you are dealing with, particularly when thinking about gender and science. For instance, there is *school science, science as a career* and the *contribution of science to society*. It is possible, for instance, to find school science interesting, see the contribution to society as positive and reject science as a career. Equally, you may find someone who finds science boring but continues with it in order to gain access to a particular career.

As far as school science is concerned, boys and girls may perform differently. For example, boys may perform better than girls at recalling information while girls have shown themselves better at handling procedural knowledge (Bell, 2001). On the other hand, girls appear to be less sceptical than boys about pseudo-scientific beliefs and superstitions, such as astrology, ghosts, palmistry, crystal power, mirror breaking (Preece and Baxter, 2000). Nevertheless, girls often do better than boys in science examinations and tend to see science as important. Girls, then, are often well-equipped to pursue science post-16 but fewer than expected do so, particularly in the physical sciences. While girls are, to some extent, under-represented in post-16 science classes, it is also true that boys are over-represented. The reasons for this are complex but, given the image of science as being a subject for men, doing science is a way of showing you are male while not doing science can be a way of showing you are female (Osborne *et al.*, 2003).

Another difference can be in the topics that interest boys and those that interest girls. Jenkins and Nelson (2005) found that boys were interested in, for example, the feeling of weightlessness, black holes, the possibility of life elsewhere, how computers work and dangerous animals. Amongst other things, girls were interested in cancer, sexually transmitted diseases, eating disorders and the effects of alcohol and tobacco. Of course, there are also topics, like the periodic table, the effects of modern farming, and patterns in leaves that seem to be disliked by both boys and girls (Osborne *et al.*, 2003; Jenkins and Nelson, 2005). It is tempting to suggest we simply omit topics that bore pupils or make them think but this would be dishonest. Science teaching is not entertainment but is an attempt, amongst other things, to show the nature of science. It may also be tempting to suggest science for girls and science for boys. However, when some female scientists were asked what attracted them to a science the reasons they gave were much the same as what might attract a man (Gilbert and Calvert, 2003). What seemed to matter more was the quality of teaching and the ability to engage learners with science. This is encouraging because teaching is in your control while topics may not be. What adds to science teaching quality? You will probably be urged to be *gender-inclusive*, that is, use both boys' *and* girls' experiences, prior knowledge and interests in your teaching. In practice, this means you need to:

- cater for different interests by tying the topic to what interests girls and boys; you may, on occasions, hook both boys' and girls' interest with something that catches their imagination equally (perhaps, 'the world's biggest germ' might do it) but often you have to dangle at least a couple of hooks, baited differently, to catch everyone's interest and point to the relevance of a topic;
- allow for changes in interest with age; the world's biggest germ may attract young pupils but could leave older ones cold; older pupils' interests may drift more towards applications of science but the same applications may not attract both boys and girls (Baram-Tsabari and Yarden, 2005); older girls may prefer structure and connections made with personal, societal and environmental issues; older boys may like to see connections made with practical devices but, usefully, this is not to say that boys have no interest in societal and environmental issues and girls have none in practical devices: it is all a matter of what interests them more at the time (Zohar, 2006);
- remember that even when both boys and girls say they like practical activity, they may like it for different reasons, or they may like different kinds or parts of practical work; boys, for instance, can like making and assembling equipment more than girls (Reid and Skryabina, 2003).

Some schools use single-sex science classes on the grounds that this makes it easier to accommodate particular interests and easier to bring about active participation, particularly on the part of girls. Some advantages have been found for this way of working (Parker and Rennie, 2002). Mixed-sex working, however, has been found to have a positive effect on liking for science (Matthews, 2004). Because the history of science is dominated by men, some have tried to update its image by having both male and female scientists talk about their work to pupils. Take care when asking scientists to talk to pupils. Not everyone is a David Bellamy who can talk enthusiastically and meaningfully to school pupils – the wrong scientist could do more harm than good. Don't forget that pupils may also see you as representing the kind of person who is interested in science.

Task 5.7 Catching interest

For one of the following topics, typical of Key Stage 4, devise or find bait for hooks to catch the interest of (a) boys, (b) girls and (c) boys and girls.

Inheritance; *or*

Enzyme effects; *or*

Mains electricity.

Discussion with colleagues can oil the wheels of creativity.

CULTURE

Each pupil who comes to you to learn science has a different history. Children grow up in different societies with different beliefs and values, which may not be like yours. Their experience is shaped by the opportunities and behaviours these beliefs and values allow and by the roles pupils are expected to take. Your pupils or their families may come from any part of the world or they may have lived in the UK for generations but come from very different social groups. Even within one social group, boys and girls may not be raised in the same way. Such differences could affect values, learning, achievement and aspirations.

For example, attitudes to science education can vary with social class. Currently, the socio-economic groups commonly known as 'middle class' show an interest in science, perhaps because it can lead to certain highly-regarded professions. So-called 'working class' pupils are said to be disinclined to take science after it ceases to be compulsory, perhaps because they do not aspire to these professions (ESRC, 2005). A little more specific is the potential for conflict between the religious beliefs of some groups and science. Pupils from a family that holds these beliefs may find the cognitive conflict difficult to cope with and so avoid the subject (Aikenhead and Jegede, 1999). Still more specific, the prior knowledge and conceptions pupils bring to science lessons reflect their experience. When you point to a concrete example to illustrate a point, it may do little for some pupils just as drawing heavily on football for your examples may leave the girls out. Referring to the Corkscrew Rule risks leaving out those who have never seen a corkscrew. And still more specific are the words you use in your science lessons. Do the pupils understand them in the way you assume they do? *Force*, for instance, has many connotations but it has a very specific one in school science that does not occur often in everyday conversation. To the extent that it is in your power to take these differences into account in your teaching, you should do so.

Some of the things to consider are:

- when you have a pupil with some aptitude, make sure that those who advise him or her on careers know of it;

- do not assume that all pupils have the same prior knowledge; it is good practice to draw out, share and explore prior knowledge whatever the nature of your class – you may find unexpected gems amongst it;
- be true to the science but be considerate when teaching topics that may lead to cognitive conflict with beliefs;
- when illustrating a point with examples, make sure they include something for everyone; when you can, have the pupils think of their own examples and share them;
- when using an analogy, check that it is meaningful to everyone; if some pupils are not familiar with it, find another or spend some time helping them become familiar with it;
- use scientific words and expressions with frequent reminders of their meaning in the specific contexts where you use them; a science dictionary kept up to date by the pupils can be useful, as can an illustrated wallchart listing and defining the scientific words used in the topic;
- whatever differences there are, pupils can also be similar; for example, learners in different parts of the world can have very similar difficulties when moving between the three worlds of chemistry: symbolic representations (e.g. equations), the sub-microscopic world (e.g. particle theory) and events in the world (e.g. the changes of state of water) (Oniru and Randell, 2006);
- listen to pupils' responses, particularly the examples they give you, and learn from them.

Task 5.8 Diversity as a resource

Your topic is energy sources, renewable and non-renewable. Use Internet resources to collect materials and pictures and prepare a 30-minute session. It should illustrate how ordinary people source their energy needs in different parts of the world. Convert the materials into a short computer-based presentation and try it out on your colleagues.

PHYSICAL DISABILITY AND MEDICAL CONDITIONS

The Disability Discrimination Act describes disability as an impairment that has lasted or is expected to last at least a year and substantially limits day-to-day activity. This description could apply to some 700,000 children of school age in Britain and others have conditions that do not 'substantially' affect activity but may have a bearing on your teaching (Mind, 2007). These include some impairment of mobility, the senses such as sight and hearing, and conditions such as asthma, colour blindness, diabetes, dyslexia, dyspraxia and epilepsy. Some are temporary, some are permanent and some may entail frequent absences from school. Disability has often reduced children's access to education, training and employment without good reason. The Act draws attention to the need for you and your school to do your best for these children.

Disabilities and medical conditions vary enormously so it is important to know what each pupil can and cannot do. This is something that the school probably has discussed with the children and their parents so ask for that information. In many cases, no special provision is needed, other than your vigilance and knowledge of what to do and who to call for help. For instance, a pupil with diabetes may need to eat or drink at some point and this may hardly affect proceedings. An epileptic seizure, on the other hand, can occur unexpectedly so you need to know what to do to prevent injury. In practice, pupils with this condition may feel that a seizure is imminent and can prevent it if you let them move away from exacerbating surroundings. Asthma may be initiated by some substance in the laboratory. If you know the trigger, you may be able to remove it.

Some conditions need more thought. Consider pupils with mobility problems. It may be that opportunities for some everyday experiences have been limited. So, for instance, it could be meaningless to draw parallels between what it feels like on a swing and the energy changes involved in pendulum motion. On the other hand, when it comes to talking about Newton's Third Law of motion, those in wheelchairs know the effects better than most.

Some conditions also need more provision. A partially sighted pupil, for instance, can benefit from a clear working space, uncluttered benches, a coloured screen to increase the contrast between the apparatus and the background, consistency in layout, and, possibly, instruments with clear, large numbers. Someone in a wheelchair may need to be higher to work at a bench or be given a lower place to work. Often, with the minimum of fuss, changes like these make doing science possible. There remains, however, the matter of safety. The activities you do have been assessed for risk but a further assessment may be needed so you can 'reduce the risk from any hazard to an acceptable level'. Take advice from your Head of Science in such cases. Only when the hazard cannot be reduced to an acceptable level can the pupil be denied access to an activity (Borrows, 2000). Ultimately, the class teacher is responsible for safety and you should clear safety requirements with that teacher on all occasions, whatever their purpose. Such occasions, however, are opportunities for you to add to your own expertise.

A final note is needed about emergency procedures, such as what to do if there is a fire alarm. A school has evacuation procedures to follow but, of course, a disabled pupil may need assistance. Be clear what to do in the event of an emergency, to ensure the safety of everyone.

Task 5.9 Making it possible

You have a pupil who has some problems with her eyesight. Her parents say she can see shapes but fine detail is blurred, particularly in low light. She has a laptop computer and uses it to write notes using a large pitch, *sans serif* script. This term, the science includes work on:

- how materials are transported through plants (their vascular system);
- acids and bases;
- the transfer of heat.

Choose one of these and think of what you would do so that this girl can make the most of the activities. How can you make it possible for her to participate *and* learn? As well as what you provide, do not neglect the opportunities provided by the laptop.

Discuss your ideas with your tutor and, if possible, with the school's special education needs coordinator.

SUMMARY

Classes are very diverse. Some examples of diversity have been described above. Teaching with variety can alleviate boredom, provide more opportunities to learn, and allow pupils to think and learn in their own ways. At the same time, it allows opportunities for you to widen a pupil's thinking and learning repertoire. The successful pupil probably already has effective ways of thinking and learning and may benefit from enrichment, extension or acceleration. The unsuccessful pupil, however, may need to take smaller learning bites, have learning highly organised, practise a lot, and be well-supported. Amongst these may be reluctant learners who may have some ability but lack motivation. Try using approaches that attract their attention and, to begin with, focus on the practical utility of the topic. Science may be seen in different ways by boys and girls, and girls may deny themselves opportunities that suit their abilities. Give thought to gender-inclusive teaching when you plan your lessons. Disability is not uncommon. Every child matters so you must do your best to make it possible for everyone to have access to a science education.

Task 5.10   A problem to solve: diversity on your doorstep

You are given some recent statistics for a class you will soon teach, and are told that 'their test results were a little disappointing'. Study the figures. What will be your priorities? How will you set about improving things?

Class characteristics (previous teacher's judgements)

	Total	Gifted	Poor learners	Reluctant learners
Boys	14	0	2	2
Girls	16	1	1	1

One of the girls has a hearing problem and sometimes explanations and instructions do not make sense to her, especially in a noisy room or when the teacher talks quickly. She was not described as a gifted, less able or reluctant learner.

Mean scores on a test of interest in school science 0 to 5 (5 = very strong interest)

All boys		3.1	All girls	2.4
			Gifted girl	2.7
Poor learners	Boys	1.9	Girls	1.3
Reluctant learners	Boys	0.5	Girls	0.6
			Girl with hearing problem	3.8

Task 5.10 *continued*

Mean test of achievement scores (%)

All boys		52	All girls	59
			(Girls without gifted girl's contribution 57)	
			Gifted girl	88
Poor learners	Boys	33	Girl	30
Reluctant learners	Boys	41	Girl	18
			Girl with hearing problem	49

(Overall means for the whole year of 120 pupils were: boys 62; girls 71.)

After you have solved the problem, and for those who want a little help, there are some brief notes on page 95.

FURTHER READING

Borrows, P. (2000) 'Teaching science to pupils with special needs – risk assessments', *School Science Review*, 81(296): 37–9.

DfES (Department for Education and Skills) (2004) *Pedagogy and Practice: teaching and learning in secondary schools*, London: DfES. You should find Units 17, 18, and 19, Developing Effective Learners, Improving the Climate for Learning, and Classroom Management, respectively, useful. At the time of writing, Unit 19, Learning Styles, is being revised.

QCA (Qualifications and Curriculum Authority) (2001) *Science: planning, teaching and assessing the curriculum for pupils with learning difficulties*, London: QCA. This offers useful advice on the subject.

Rodrigues. S., Airnes, J. and Powell, M. (undated) *Ideas for Using Television Fiction in Science Classrooms*, and *Teachers Using Television Fiction in Science Classroom* (undated), Edinburgh University: The Institute for Science Education in Scotland. (Institute for Science Education in Scotland, University of Edinburgh, The Old Faculty Office Building, The King's Buildings, West Mains Road, Edinburgh, EH9 3JY.) The second item was prepared by experienced teachers and exemplifies the approach.

Thompson, M. (2006) *Supporting Gifted and Talented Pupils in the Secondary School*, London: Paul Chapman. This has relevance for the teaching of very able pupils.

Chapter 6   Some broader aspects of science teaching

All you need to do to receive guidance is to ask for it then listen.

Sanaya Roman

INTRODUCTION

There are some broader aspects of science that need your attention. These relate to matters that cross subject boundaries. For instance, you know that moving from one school to another is a difficult time for some pupils so you try to do your bit to smooth the transfer and transition. Sound thinking is encouraged in all subjects and that developed in science is a contribution to pupils' skills. ICT skills are developed and applied in many subjects and those cultivated in science help to equip your pupils for the role of ICT in life as well as in science. It is not only skill that crosses subject boundaries. Knowledge of sustainable development, for instance, is covered in several subjects and you contribute to it in science. And, of course, the personal development of pupils is a matter for several teachers so you would expect to contribute to that, amongst other things. By the end of the chapter you should:

- know some examples of teaching you will share with others, such as, those relating to transfers and transitions, thinking skills, education for sustainable development, personal development, and ICT skills;
- know how to make a contribution to these areas in your science lessons.

This being the final chapter, it concludes with some brief thoughts on:

- your own professional development and support for it.

TRANSFER AND TRANSITION

Life is full of change and school life is no exception. Transitions from one school year to another and between Key Stages within one school can be fairly smooth. You generally know in detail what last year's work entailed and how it was taught, and you may have taught the pupils before. Transfers from one place to somewhere else, to different teachers who work in different ways, and sometimes without your friends, can be disturbing. These most commonly occur *en masse* when moving from the primary school to the secondary school and from the Sixth Form to university, although it is also common for some pupils to transfer from a secondary school to a Sixth Form Centre and, in some areas, from a Middle School to High

School. Of course, transfers may occur at any time when pupils move between schools for a variety of reasons.

Details of each child's performance are commonly passed between schools and Year 6 children are usually prepared for the move in order to lessen their anxieties. Nevertheless, the primary to secondary transition is associated with a significant dip in progress that is evident by the end of Year 7. At least some of this has been ascribed to a failure to pick up where the primary school left off and to recognise that young pupils take time to become used to different ways of teaching and learning (e.g. Hargreaves and Galton, 2002). Some teachers still cling to the idea of a 'fresh start' in Year 7 although the National Curriculum is intended to progress smoothly from 5 to 16 years. The temptation is understandable, given that a Year 7 teacher may have pupils from several feeder schools with different backgrounds. Equally understandable is young pupils' boredom with repetition and 'making sure' of existing knowledge.

Task 6.1 As others see us

'I know that the teachers are still settling in, but I'm still waiting for the hard work.' This is one girl's comment some time after a transfer (Transfer and Transition Project, 2003: 5).

What does it tell you?

How would you build on such a pupil's earlier learning and give her what she wants?

Compare your thoughts with those of your colleagues.

One strategy to help children cross the divide is the *bridging topic*. This is when a science topic, such as Force and Flight or Lifecycles or The Environment is started in the primary school, usually after the SATs have been completed. The children then take their work to their first science classes in the secondary school to be developed further and completed. In the topic The Environment, for example, Year 6 children may examine habitats, identify organisms using a simple key and construct a key themselves. They take this work with them into Year 7 where they describe and measure variables in habitats and study animal adaptation (Braund and Hames, 2005). In Year 7, teaching approaches familiar to the children are used. For instance, you might begin with a review of the last lesson, draw out prior knowledge and use it to lead into this lesson, set tasks which are differentiated to suit children of different abilities and end with a plenary session that brings ideas together. There is nothing new in this: it is simply good practice (DfES, 2004). Included in this, however, is a transition to new ways of learning. Children are encouraged to think about how to improve and manage their learning (sometimes referred to as metacognition, the self-regulation of learning and study skills). Other strategies concern themselves with lessening the risk that children with learning difficulties fall so far behind that they find it easier to give up. So, for instance, they may attend a summer school to prepare them for the changes. If you recall your first year at university, there are some parallels, particularly in some pupils' inability to cope with self-directed learning. You might bear this in mind if you have a Sixth Form class and try to help them develop self-directed learning skills.

Task 6.2   New kids on the block

Your new class arrives from the primary school. Think about how the children feel. What would you have liked to see, hear and do in your first science lesson? What would have sent you away wanting more?

Prepare a skeleton or outline plan for these pupils' first lesson on a topic of your choice.

Your colleagues' or tutor's thoughts on what this lesson should be like could be useful.

DEVELOPING THINKING SKILLS

Learning involves thought and, with practice, some thinking may be improved. Accordingly, we exercise the pupils' minds with:

- storing and recalling, making mental connections and understanding information;
- comparing, contrasting, reasoning, evaluating evidence, drawing conclusions, and otherwise manipulating information;
- applying, predicting, theorising, hypothesising, investigating, creating ideas, and problem solving.

The question is, can we do more than provide practice? There is evidence that bringing these thought processes out into the open – thinking and talking about thinking – can give pupils:

- a vocabulary about thinking for them to use;
- an awareness of the thinking that is relevant in a given context;
- a wider repertoire of thinking tools;
- some proficiency in efficient and effective thought.

In short, specific advice coupled with practice can make a difference to thinking, especially in science and mathematics (Marzano, 1998).

How might you have your pupils think and talk about their thinking? Suppose, for example, you were teaching about floating and sinking. You show the pupils a stone and ask what will happen if you drop stones into a dish of water. They will predict that the stones will sink. You ask why and they explain that it is because stones are heavy and heavy things sink. You have ready some sets of stones. In each set is a piece of pumice and amongst the other stones in the set is one of the same mass and another of the same volume as the pumice. The set also includes some stones that are larger and smaller than the pumice. You drop the set of stones into the dish. To their puzzlement, the pumice does not sink. You point out that this is not what they predicted. Something must be wrong. You ask if it could be their idea that heavy things sink. As you expected, they are reluctant to abandon what has been for them a useful rule and you assign them to groups, give them pencil and paper and a set of stones and invite them to solve the problem. You instruct them to write the problem in the centre of the sheet, examine the stones and think of a solution. The pupils 'weigh' the stones by hand and quickly conclude that the pumice is unusually light for a stone and that is why it floats. You draw attention to other stones that are palpably lighter than the pumice yet they sink. Why don't they float? It looks like their rule doesn't always get it right. Why is that? Each group generates ideas. To help them explore their thoughts, you make available a dish of water, scales, and a measuring cylinder. After one or two false starts, their new rule is that big, lightweight stones may float but heavy, small stones are likely to sink.

You bring the groups together to review matters. First, you ask what their sinking rule was to start with and what it predicted. Then you remind them that here is a stone that didn't do what their rule said it should. You ask what this tells them about their rule. You then ask them to remind you of the purpose of their group work and take you through their thinking. What did they do first? What next? Why? What did they find out? You have them express it in different ways and tidy their new rule up a little, perhaps using terms like, 'light for its size'. Finally, you have them apply their new rule by asking them how they might make any stone 'light for its size' so it will float. Their new rule points to *two* ways: they could hollow stones out to make them lighter or they could increase their volume by attaching balloons. You could also describe the ballast tanks of a submarine and ask how they are used to make it heavy for its size and then light for its size. A review which exercises your pupils' vocabulary about thinking, has them reflect on it, note what is effective and share thinking tools is potentially useful. It makes it evident that thinking skills are not fixed forever at some predetermined level but may be extended or made more effective or efficient with practice.

There are various programmes intended to help pupils develop their thinking. Generally, programmes that aim to develop skills though a subject rather than in isolation are found to be more effective. Cognitive Acceleration through Science Education (CASE) is one of these. It uses science activities to stimulate cognitive conflict (as with the puzzlement produced by a floating stone, described above). These activities oblige a pupil to think, reflect and apply ideas in new contexts. The effect is to increase reasoning ability and produce higher GCSE grades, not just in science but also in mathematics and English. As a result, CASE has attracted the attention of schools as a way of raising standards (Adey *et al.*, 1995; Adey and Shayer, 1994). The application of the skills in scientific investigation is obvious (Jones and Gott, 1998) but the benefits are meant to extend across the breadth of science learning.

At times, topics can be cast in the form of a problem. In the example above, for instance, you would ask pupils to predict what would happen when the piece of pumice was placed in water. When they say it will sink, you show that it floats and ask, 'Why is that? Why doesn't this stone sink like other stones do?' You might display responses on the board in the form of a concept cartoon and then challenge them to solve the problem. Problem solving is practised in several subjects so using it in science adds experience and variety. Note that problem solving is essentially a creative process. Imagination is exercised in creating potential explanations and in devising scientific tests of them. Matters of safety, however, must always be considered. Your pupils may devise unexpected ways to test their ideas so check them and have them approved before they are tried. Some of their ideas may have to be tested in a later lesson, so have some back-up ideas just in case they are needed.

Task 6.3 Being thoughtful

Suppose you have to teach a lesson about reaction rates and your lesson agenda is as follows:

1   Recall and interest. (Picture of decayed limestone carving on a building. Ask why it gets like this and how long it takes. Recall or show action of acid on limestone chips.)
2   Problem. (How long does the chips' reaction take? Is it over quickly? Explain 'rate of reaction' as amount going on per minute. Ask how to measure the rate of reaction.)
3   Demonstration. (Rate of reaction: flask containing limestone chips on balance; dilute hydrochloric acid added and loose cotton wool placed in neck of flask to stop acid droplets; starting mass and time noted; mass taken every minute until reaction is negligible. NB Check safety precautions.)
4   Graphing activity. (Pupils draw graph of mass against time. Discuss meaning of graph; identify the rate of reaction at various times. Ask what might make the reaction rate different.)
5   Review and sum up. (Ask what this activity suggests about the conditions that make limestone carvings decay. How might they test their suggestions in the next lesson?)

Where does this give you a chance to model thinking (thinking aloud)?

Where might you talk about the thinking of your pupils?

EDUCATION FOR SUSTAINABLE DEVELOPMENT

There are some important themes that run through several school subjects. Sustainable development is one. Sustainable development is about how we should meet our material needs without making it unduly difficult for others and for future generations. Education for Sustainable Development (ESD) aims to show your pupils the need for ways of living and working that do not degrade the environment. It also prepares them for decisions that will affect the way they live and, consequently, the way subsequent generations live. There are seven aspects of ESD:

- citizenship and stewardship;
- sustainable change;
- needs and rights of future generations;
- interdependence;
- diversity;
- uncertainty and precaution;
- quality of life, equity and justice.

None of this means you have more science to teach. Instead, it means that when you teach a science topic that relates to sustainability, you could use it as a *context* for the science. For example, suppose your topic is to do with the transmission of heat. A popular sustainability matter is the need to reduce heat loss from houses in order to reduce fuel consumption, heating bills, and carbon dioxide production. After introducing the problem, your pupils could investigate materials they might use to insulate a loft or compare the effects of single and double glazing (a beaker of warm water compared with one nested inside another beaker). To widen their science, you might show and discuss a picture of an eco-house with its wind generator, solar panels, insulation and light pipes to illuminate rooms with natural light.

Alternatively, you could use the science as a *conduit* that leads to a sustainability issue. When you teach about purifying water, for example, you could point out that drinking water can be in short supply, even in the UK. In Qatar, people are encouraged to live by the sea where the sun's heat is used to distil sea water. What could a solar still look like? Tying the science to the real world like this can add interest (but remember that boys' and girls' interests may not coincide). It shows that real-world problems are complex, that what someone does in one place may affect others elsewhere, and that we may have more opinions than facts so we must think cautiously. These matters touch upon several of the key aspects of ESD listed above.

You are not the only person developing ESD. Because other subjects, such as geography, design and technology and history can contribute to ESD, schools generally work out who does what and will probably have made someone responsible for a programme. In addition, there may be school-wide ESD events which put into practice some of what you and others teach. So, for instance, your pupils may be involved in activities to reduce energy costs or to reduce the amount of non-recyclable waste in school. Pupil involvement in projects like this can make their learning more meaningful and durable.

Task 6.4 Leading the way to ESD

Consider one of the following science topics as a conduit for teaching about ESD. What ESD matters might they lead to? Also identify the key aspects of ESD it would support (see the list above). The hints are merely possibilities. You may have better ideas.

Task 6.4 *continued*

- genetics (hint: genetic modification and disease resistant crops):

- properties of materials (hint: bio- and non-biodegradable materials):

- expansion of materials due to heat (hint: sea water and global warming):

Such topics can lead to a variety of sustainable development matters. Compare your ideas with those of a colleague or work together.

Task 6.5 Two birds with one stone

Suppose you had to teach about:

- food as a source of energy in biology; *or*
- energy sources in chemistry; *or*
- measuring energy in physics.

How would you use ESD to provide an interesting context or starting point? Prepare some ideas to share with a colleague and then work together on an agreed agenda.

CITIZENSHIP, PERSONAL, SOCIAL, MORAL, SPIRITUAL, CULTURAL AND HEALTH EDUCATION (CPSHE)

Education for Sustainable Development is an example of cross-curricular learning where the contribution of science is relatively clear. Schools, however, make provision for other cross-curricular learning in such areas as CPSHE. This net catches a variety of matters which can change or evolve with time. In state schools, the topic of sex education and relationships is included. Generally, schools have a programme that sets out how opportunities are provided. These may be timetabled and taught by a designated person on a regular basis, perhaps using a commercial scheme and textbooks. As with ESD, science can be a vehicle to make a contribution (Jenkins, 1999).

You may find it relatively easy to see opportunities for a contribution. For instance, you may have to teach about health and balanced diets, the effect of drugs and alcohol abuse, the causes of disease and disease control, reproduction, sound and noise, nuclear power, and the effects of electromagnetic radiation as a part of the National Curriculum. Each has a bearing on current problems such as obesity, anorexia, beliefs about cannabis use, measles and mumps vaccination, bird 'flu, venereal disease and contraception, the siting of airport runways, the disposal of nuclear waste, and the potential effects of sunbathing. Science can say something about each of these. However, when you do so, you have moved much closer to the concerns, fears and beliefs of your pupils. Talking about what matters a lot to them can capture their interest but it needs sensitivity and caution. You may, for instance, notice pupils who are over- or underweight and you may be aware that some parents hold religious views about contraception, but you are much less likely to know of a parent who is being treated for skin cancer.

For your early contributions, choose a 'safe' topic that is less likely to involve sensitive issues. You may opt for noise pollution, road traffic and the quality of the environment. Your pupils could investigate noise intensity and compare measured loudness and perceptions of loudness. You make the point that perceptions are not always objective and ask if perceptions matter. This introduces values, the quality of life and the need for transport and employment that, together, make the problem complex. Then there is the matter of one person's noise is another person's music, which leads to issues of rights and responsibilities.

As you gain in confidence, you might try other kinds of topic. In Key Stage 3, you are likely to teach about healthy eating and living and introduce the problem of obesity and anorexia. It is important to teach the correct terminology to facilitate discussion. Words may be listed on the board and the pupils referred to them. Have a clear goal or end point and state that, too. You may need to set out ground rules for discussion and should know clearly what you will say and do if discussion goes in inappropriate or personal directions. If in doubt, ask a more experienced colleague for advice. You find, with a little practice, that you soon get the hang of it and, in the process, add a valuable teaching skill to your repertoire (Levinson, 2005a; Maloney, 2005).

As with ESD, topics to do with CPSHE may be a starting point for science or the science may be a starting point for the topic. As with any teaching session, plan carefully what you do and how you handle it. Do not try to teach it off the cuff. There are also websites with useful background information that give you a feel for what is appropriate (e.g. www.mindbody soul.gov.uk and www.lifebytes.gov.uk/teachers).

Task 6.6 A special interest

Choose a topic that connects with an aspect of CPSHE. For example, you might choose from: health and diet; reproduction; disease and disease control; drugs, alcohol and solvents; sound and noise.

Make this your specialist topic. Explore it using a variety of sources. List the science in it and, next to the list, spell out the connections with CPSHE. Highlight parts that may prove to be sensitive.

Now plan or discuss with colleagues or your tutor how you would make the connections in the classroom.

INFORMATION AND COMMUNICATIONS TECHNOLOGY (ICT) IN SCIENCE EDUCATION

ICT capability is also developed across subjects. First, you should distinguish between ICT as a subject and ICT in subjects (DfES, 2004). The former is about the skills, knowledge and understanding of ICT. Schools are recommended to provide separate time to teach these in Key Stage 3. Where the science scheme of work mentions specific activities involving ICT, it reflects what has been covered in this Key Stage. Otherwise, look at the ICT programme yourself so you know what the pupils can handle. ICT in science largely involves using ICT to support learning and using ICT as a tool. There can be some overlap between the two.

ICT to support learning involves, for instance:

1 Seeking, selecting and organising information using software and particular websites that you identify (and supervise, to avoid inappropriate sites) and using an interactive whiteboard.

- This can allow pupils to work at their own pace, take their own route through the material, and work at a level suited to them. Some software is better at supporting this than others.

2 Seeing and/or interacting with simulations of events, virtual experiments and models.

- Some phenomena, events and practical work are dangerous or inaccessible but ICT can let pupils see them in virtual laboratories. So, for instance, reactions like that of caesium and water or of hydrogen and fluorine can be observed safely. ICT can also make the invisible visible through animated models and microworlds, as when a pupil observes a depiction of a current in a circuit or interacts with a model of home energy use to maintain a constant temperature while minimising fuel consumption. Some have pointed to the time saved in 'doing' experiments in this way (DfES, 2004). Used for work that can safely be undertaken in school, however, ICT removes the pupil from manipulating equipment, experiencing the real world and finding out that things do not always go as expected.

Using ICT as a tool involves, for example:

1 Preparing information for a presentation (e.g. using Powerpoint), entering data in a spreadsheet and processing them, graphing data to see patterns, writing an account of an investigation.

- Having the computer do number crunching and produce graphs frees pupils to think about the point of an activity. On the other hand, those not already able to handle these manually need to practise them at some point.

2 Capturing data using various sensors, monitoring and controlling experiments and devices (e.g. logging temperature and/or pH of reacting substances at certain intervals of time.)

- Again, these can free a pupil to focus on what matters in the event.

Pupils can find working with ICT in these ways motivating. It often lets them make mistakes in private and allows them to review or revise earlier material as often as they wish (Kennewell, 2004; Wellington, 2004; Osborne and Hennessy, 2006). For success, you need to be familiar with the software and know when it is better to do things in other ways.

Task 6.7 ICT to support learning

Consider one of the following topics and find one or more websites you could use to supplement your teaching at Key Stage 3. Be clear what it is that the pupils would do when visiting the sites:

- living things in their environment; *or*
- geological changes; *or*
- the Earth and beyond.

Add the information to your useful ideas collection for future use.

Task 6.8 ICT as a tool

For some aspect of one of the following topics, consider how you would use ICT as a tool in practical work at Key Stage 4:

- living things in their environment; *or*
- chemical reactions; *or*
- radioactivity.

Make a note of the resources you need and the information you collect and file it for future use.

CONTINUING PROFESSIONAL DEVELOPMENT (CPD)

As a teacher, you are expected to move with the times and show progress yourself. See keeping up to date as a part of the job. Never let your teaching stagnate. Look for opportunities to attend further training courses, perhaps at your nearest Science Learning Centre. Listen to what is going on in other schools and keep an eye on websites that support CPD (such as www.teachernet.gov.uk/professionaldevelopment and www.gtce.org.uk). Perhaps you might also like to join the Association for Science Education (www.ase.org.uk) which can help you keep up to date through its publications, resources and meetings.

In the meantime, see what you can do for yourself. Thinking about your teaching can help it improve. One way is to add a note to your lesson plan saying how well it went. But don't leave it at that. Jot down why it went well or why it did not go as planned and decide what you will do differently next time (Capel *et al.*, 2005: Unit 5.4). As a new teacher, you are likely to be given a mentor to guide you. Your mentor can help you learn the ropes quickly. Some of the things you need to know are fairly mundane and straightforward: where the pens for overhead projector transparencies are kept, what is expected of you in school assemblies, how parents' evenings operate. But your mentor may also be able to help you with other professional matters, such as an approach to try with a difficult class or pupil, how to provide information for parents, or how to prepare for an inspection or annual review. A colleague or mentor may sit in a lesson occasionally and give you some feedback on your teaching. It may be possible to video record a lesson discreetly for you to study in private. You are a member of a team and, as the quote said at the outset, all you have to do is ask.

Of course, there is more job satisfaction if you maintain your own interest in what you do. As your expertise grows, you may become bored with a lesson. If that happens, change it in some way. Make something different each year and make it something to look forward to. Try to make your teaching more engaging and more successful so that you feel rewarded. This means looking at how you might:

- plan, teach and manage the class better;
- monitor, assess, record and report information better.

Another aspect of ICT that is worth a thought is what it can do for your lesson plans. One of the great pleasures of teaching is giving a good lesson and seeing your pupils make progress. There are websites with ideas to help you prepare a good lesson, such as TeacherNet (www. teachernet.gov.uk), National Curriculum in Action (www.ncaction.org.uk) and the British Educational Communications and Technology Agency (www.becta.org.uk/). Learn to pluck the gems from such sources so that you end up with a lesson in tune with your pupils' needs and interests. Add to these some of your own gems. Be creative with lesson plans: trying out new ideas can be rewarding and adds interest to your teaching throughout your working life.

As your experience and skills develop, opportunities present themselves for advancement so be in a position to take those that attract you (Levinson, 2005b). Think about what you can contribute in your school to increase its effectiveness. At the same time, try to remember what starting out is like so that you, in turn, can be a useful tutor and mentor for those who follow. Good luck!

Task 6.9 Adding to your skills

Use the Internet to find out about Science Learning Centres, funded initially by the Wellcome Trust and the government. What do they do? What other sources of continuing professional development are there? What is going on out there which might help you teach science better?

Record this information in your database or collection of useful materials.

SUMMARY

Some aspects of your work as a science teacher are shared with other teachers. You contribute to cross-curricular concerns, such as thinking skills, ESD, ICT, citizenship, social, moral, spiritual, cultural and personal development and have a regard for times when pupils may not make the progress they should, such as after a school transfer. In addition, your school has its own concerns, which you must support. For example, there may be a problem with bullying and all teachers are expected to help solve the problem. Learning how to meet such expectations makes it a busy time, an interesting one and a rewarding one, particularly if you continue to learn yourself.

Task 6.10   A problem to solve: what counts as a good performance?

As a part of the induction process or in the cycle of performance management in school, you should expect to have the quality of your teaching appraised. Eventually, you may have to sit in someone's lesson and appraise it yourself. What would you look for? Construct an appraisal pro-forma you would use. The 'scaffold' below is to start your thinking. You add your own ideas and can have more or fewer items under each heading.

You could find it useful to talk to a tutor about the kinds of things that matter in their appraisals and what, for instance, Ofsted inspectors look for. It may help to work with a colleague or ask your tutor to comment on the list.

The purpose of the lesson

What is the teacher trying to achieve in this lesson?

Is it an appropriate goal for these pupils?

Rating (5 = excellent)

Planning

1 2 3 4 5

1 _____ ❑ ❑ ❑ ❑ ❑

2 _____ ❑ ❑ ❑ ❑ ❑

3 _____ ❑ ❑ ❑ ❑ ❑

4 _____ ❑ ❑ ❑ ❑ ❑

5 _____ ❑ ❑ ❑ ❑ ❑

Delivery

Beginning the lesson

1 _____ ❑ ❑ ❑ ❑ ❑

2 _____ ❑ ❑ ❑ ❑ ❑

3 _____ ❑ ❑ ❑ ❑ ❑

4 _____ ❑ ❑ ❑ ❑ ❑

5 _____ ❑ ❑ ❑ ❑ ❑

Task 6.10 *continued*

The core of the lesson

1 _____ ☐☐☐☐☐

2 _____ ☐☐☐☐☐

3 _____ ☐☐☐☐☐

4 _____ ☐☐☐☐☐

5 _____ ☐☐☐☐☐

6 _____ ☐☐☐☐☐

7 _____ ☐☐☐☐☐

8 _____ ☐☐☐☐☐

9 _____ ☐☐☐☐☐

10 _____ ☐☐☐☐☐

Ending the lesson

1 _____ ☐☐☐☐☐

2 _____ ☐☐☐☐☐

3 _____ ☐☐☐☐☐

4 _____ ☐☐☐☐☐

5 _____ ☐☐☐☐☐

Other matters, as appropriate: e.g. cross curricular work and inclusivity (such as matters of gender, culture, high and low ability)

1 _____ ☐☐☐☐☐

2 _____ ☐☐☐☐☐

3 _____ ☐☐☐☐☐

4 _____ ☐☐☐☐☐

5 _____ ☐☐☐☐☐

Summing up

To what extent was the goal achieved?

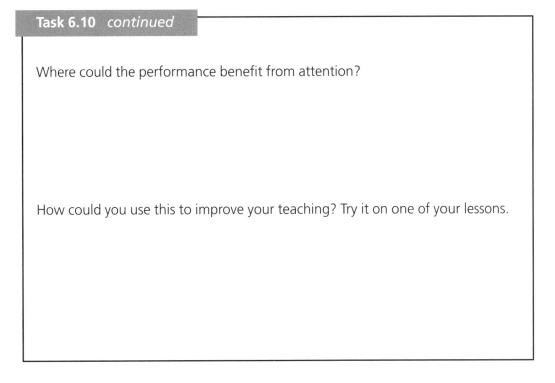

Task 6.10 *continued*

Where could the performance benefit from attention?

How could you use this to improve your teaching? Try it on one of your lessons.

After you have solved the problem and for those who want a little help, there are some brief notes on page 95.

FURTHER READING

DfES (Department for Education and Skills) (2004) *Pedagogy and Practice: teaching and learning in secondary schools*, London: DfES. You may find Units 5, 9, and 10, 'Starters and Plenaries', 'Guided Learning', and 'Group Work', useful when thinking about supporting a class after a transfer from feeder schools. Similarly, Units 2 and 17, 'Teaching models' and 'Developing effective learners', could be useful for helping pupils acquire some thinking and learning skills. Unit 15 is about using ICT to enhance learning.

Levinson, R. (2005a) 'Science for citizenship', in J. Frost and T. Turner (eds), *Learning to Teach Science in the Secondary School: a companion to school experience*, 2nd edn, Abingdon: RoutledgeFalmer, 251–69. This is an excellent contribution to the teaching of cross-curricular matters.

Maloney, J. (2005) 'Sex and health education', in J. Frost and T. Turner (eds), *Learning to Teach Science in the Secondary School: a companion to school experience*, 2nd edn, Abingdon: RoutledgeFalmer, 270–81. This practical account is recommended for helping you teach about sex and health education.

Ofsted (2003) *Taking the first step forward towards an education for sustainable development*, HMI 1658, London: Ofsted. Available at www.ofsted.gov.uk. To learn more about ESD try Unesco (2002) *Teaching and Learning for a Sustainable Future*, www.unesco.org/education/dsf.

Wellington, J. (2004) 'Multimedia in science teaching', in R. Barton (ed.) *Teaching Secondary Science with ICT*, Oxford: Oxford University Press. This is a useful source on ICT use in science education.

Appendix   **A problem to solve**

Some notes on the activities at
the end of each chapter

TASK 1.10 (PAGE 16)

It sounds like these pupils lack a knowledge base to think with. They would benefit from some preliminary teaching to give them concepts and structures relating to habitats and ecosystems. This preparation would enable them to think about the task in non-trivial ways. It also seems that Roger did not support the pupils in their work by, for example, asking questions to shape thought. Furthermore, doing one kind of activity every lesson can become tedious, particularly when the point is being missed.

TASK 2.10 (PAGE 30)

The plan (or, at least, the underlying idea of engaging pupils in the work) seems to have some potential. Mr Ward's oversight regarding differences in prior knowledge made it difficult for engaging, interesting work to take place: even experienced teachers can make mistakes. Would it have been possible to retrieve the situation? Mr Ward may have divided the class into groups according to prior knowledge. Each group would then engage with tasks that suited their knowledge. Such a change would have called for additional work by Mr Ward, and it can be tempting to stick with what you have prepared, even though it is failing.

TASK 3.10 (PAGE 47)

It also looks like Dawn did not prepare the way well enough at the beginning of the lesson, and the result was that the demonstration was undertaken before the pupils had much grasp of prerequisite ideas. Presumably Dawn tried the reaction beforehand, so she should have anticipated some doubtful responses and been ready for them. The activity at the end would not do much to clarify matters. This seemed a rather hurried lesson that needed better pacing, some clear, concrete examples of mixtures and compounds, a clear statement of the purpose of the demonstration, and a better concluding task. What might these be?

TASK 4.10 (PAGE 63)

Twenty minutes to assess a topic is not a long time. If you intend to cover the topic reasonably well, you might use a mix of multiple choice and short answer questions. If so, you might begin with recall questions and move to more demanding, productive thought questions. This allows everyone a chance to demonstrate what they have achieved and can do.

TASK 5.10 (PAGE 77)

One approach would be to identify the 'core' of the class, that is the ten boys and thirteen girls who were neither gifted nor altogether unsuccessful learners. This core showed, at best, an indifference to science and a relatively low level of achievement. You could draft plans with that in mind. Next, you might look at the unsuccessful learners and adjust your plan. Consider now what to do about the gifted girl. Will you give her more demanding work or a personal project, or will you wait a short while? Now, consider the girl with a hearing problem and more interest in science than most in the class. How will you ensure she has the opportunity to achieve her potenial? Also ask yourself if she has some untapped potential. How would you know?

TASK 6.10 (PAGE 91)

If you skim through summaries of the six chapters, you will find ideas for what might appear in your list. You could ask someone to use your proforma to assess one of your lessons, or use it yourself on one that has been video recorded.

Glossary

Alternative conception A knowledge or explanation of some aspect of the world that is not commonly held by scientists at the present time. Alternative conceptions can shape thought in big ways, as when someone believes that medical diagnosis is a sure process. Misconceptions are similar, although the term alternative conceptions is favoured by some because it does not carry connotations of error. Some simply call it prior knowledge.

Analogy An analogy is a familiar object or process that is used to explain something less familiar and often invisible to the human eye. It is one of a class of devices (including metaphors, similes, models, examples) commonly used to aid thinking and memory.

Big ideas These are scientific ideas that have been successful in explaining a wide range of phenomena; they include, for instance, evolution, the particulate theory of matter and wave theory.

Bridging Bridging is the provision of a set of teaching steps that lead from what is known to what is to be learned. It may also describe an activity started in a primary school and continued in a secondary school to smooth the transition from the first school to the second.

Cognitive acceleration A term referring to a desired outcome of certain teaching interventions. The teaching is generally intended to improve the quality of thinking faster than commonly occurs, as in the CASE project.

Cognitive conflict This refers to the effect of seeing something that contradicts expectations. Learners with cognitive conflict may be stimulated to resolve the conflict by revising the rules or theories that produce the expectations. This suggests a strategy for teaching a topic where misconceptions or alternative conceptions are present.

Concept cartoon A pictorial depiction, usually of a scientific problem, with pupils' explanations added.

Creativity in science This is evident when ideas are generated to produce, for instance, an explanation or to construct an experimental test.

Critical thinking Thinking that questions assumptions and identifies strengths and weaknesses in reasoning. It is not being negative about everything: critical thinking can lead to agreement with an argument.

Cross-curricular matters Aspects of teaching and learning that are not confined to only one subject. Thinking skills and Education for Sustainable Development are examples.

Differentiation The modification of a task or experience provided to suit different kinds or levels of ability.

Dyslexia An impairment in the ability to read not caused by low intelligence. An old term for this was 'word-blindness'.

Dyspraxia An impairment in the ability to perform deliberate actions, producing a kind of clumsiness.

Empirical Based on observation of the world or on experiment.

Feedback Information about achievement and advice intended to support further learning. It may also be described as formative feedback, in which the intention is to shape further development.

Focused questioning Questions tailored to help pupils think about what matters in different parts of a lesson.

Forced prediction Questions that ask a pupil to make a prediction after the pupil has been given information to understand. To comply, the pupil must first construct something meaningful with the information.

Formative assessment Assessing learning in order to help the pupil improve, generally by providing feedback on the strengths and weakness of the performance and advice on how to build on strengths and overcome weaknesses.

Gender inclusive Teaching that draws on and extends boys' *and* girls' experiences, knowledge and interests and allows for diverse ways of thinking, learning and working.

Gifted A term used to describe pupils who are very able in one or more subjects. The term tends to be used in subjects like mathematics and science, while *talented* tends to be used in subjects like music and art.

Higher level thinking An expression used to refer to the thinking involved in understanding, explaining, reasoning, justifying, predicting, relating and critical appraisal, as opposed to the thinking associated with rote learning.

Learning difficulty Pupils who experience a significant and persistent impediment to learning.

Learning style A learning style is a more or less consistent way of thinking and learning. A large number of learning style systems have been postulated. Some lack a firm basis and evidential support.

Metacognition Thinking about your thinking, generally in order to improve its effectiveness.

Misconception See 'alternative conceptions'.

Mnemonic A mnemonic is a memory aid, usually using something familiar or easily learned to reconstruct something less familiar or not easily brought to mind.

Model of teaching A model of teaching exemplifies the teaching process. Models of teaching vary in usefulness. An experienced, skilled teacher would be a good model. Textbooks may also serve as convenient models for some aspects of teaching. They, too, vary in quality.

Pedagogical knowledge A teacher's knowledge of how science can be taught. It encompasses, for instance, knowledge of activities suited to different kinds of learner, ways of describing and explaining aspects of science, analogies and examples, class management routines, and particular ways of assessing science learning.

Problem solving An approach that presents what is to be learned as a scientific problem; possible solutions (usually possible explanations) are generally investigated practically. Problem solving skills are valued and practised across subjects.

Public examination An examination set by a body that is independent of and external to the school. Well known in the UK are SATs, the GCSE and A-level examinations.

Reluctant learners Pupils who may have the ability to learn but prefer to avoid it.

Risk assessment Carried out to determine the nature and magnitude of hazards in an activity with the aim of reducing them to an acceptable level.

Scientific knowledge Knowledge of scientific products, such as concepts, laws, principles and theories, and knowledge of scientific processes that produce these products.

Scientific literacy At its simplest, this term refers to the knowledge of science a pupils might acquire to equip them for adult life in general. In practice, what this knowledge should constitute is debatable.

Self-regulation of learning The control of the learning process by the learner. This is a necessary skill for times when the teacher does not control or manage learning for the pupil.

Study skills The skills a learner has that help him or her to engage in learning effectively and efficiently.

Summative assessment The assessment of learning in order to have an indication of pupils' quantity and quality of learning at a particular stage.

Target setting This refers to the process of arriving at agreed goals and, commonly, the actions needed to achieve them.

Theory A theory is a potential explanation of some aspect of the world; to be scientific, a theory has to be at least testable in principle.

Thinking skills The skills of processing information mentally. There is evidence that managing skill use is something that can be improved through metacognition, or thinking about thinking.

Value-added A term used to describe the gain in learning of a pupil or group of pupils over a period of time.

Word bank This is a list of words relating to the topic in hand. Pupils may be asked to choose the correct word from it (or use the words in their answers).

References

Adey, P.S. and Shayer, M. (1994) *Really Raising Standards*, London: Routledge.

Adey, P.S., Shayer, M. and Yates, C. (1995) *Thinking Science: the Materials of the CASE Project*, London: Nelson.

Aikenhead, G.S. and Jegede, O. (1999) 'Cross-cultural science education', *Journal of Research in Science Teaching*, 36(3), 269–87.

Amos, S. and Boohan, R. (eds) (2002) *Aspects of Teaching Secondary Science*, London: RoutledgeFalmer.

ASE (Association for Science Education) (2006a) *Science Education in Schools: issues, evidence and proposals*, Hatfield: ASE.

ASE (Association for Science Education) (2006b) *Safeguards in the School Laboratory*, Hatfield: ASE.

Baram-Tsabari, A. and Yarden, A. (2005) 'Characterising children's spontaneous interests in science and technology', *International Journal of Science Education*, 27(7), 803–26.

Bell, J.F. (2001) 'Investigating gender differences in the science performance of 16-year-old pupils in the UK', *International Journal of Science Education*, 23(5), 499–86.

Bennett, J. (2003) *Teaching and Learning Science*, London: Continuum.

Bettencourt, E.M., Gillet, M.H. and Gall, M.D. (1983) 'Effects of teacher enthusiasm on student on-task behavior and achievement', *American Educational Research Journal*, 20, 435–50.

Bleeker, M.M. and Jacobs, J.E. (2004) 'Achievement in math and science', *Journal Of Educational Psychology*, 96(1), 97–109.

Borrows, P. (1998) 'Safety in science education', in M. Ratcliffe (ed.), *ASE Guide to Secondary Science Education*, Hatfield: Stanley Thornes/ASE, 183–91.

Borrows, P. (2000) 'Teaching science to pupils with special needs – risk assessments', *School Science Review*, 81(296), 37–9.

Braund, M. and Hames, V. (2005) 'Improving progression and continuity from primary to secondary school: pupils' reactions to bridging work', *International Journal of Science Education*, 27(7), 781–801.

Capel, S., Leask, M. and Turner, T. (eds) (2005) *Learning to Teach in the Secondary School: a companion to school experience*, 4th edn, Abingdon: RoutledgeFalmer.

Carlsen, W. (1991) 'Subject matter knowledge and science teaching', in J.E. Brophy (ed.), *Advances in Research on Teaching*, vol. 2, Greenwich: JAI Press, 115–43.

Cerbin, B. (2000) 'Learning with and teaching for understanding', Background paper prepared for the Wisconsin Teaching Fellows Summer Institute, 24 July–3 August.

CLEAPSS (Consortium of Local Education Authorities for the Provision of Science Services) (2004) 'Health and safety in the school laboratory and the new science teacher.' Available online: www.cleapss.org.uk.

Cleaves, A. (2005) 'The formation of science choices in secondary school', *International Journal of Science Education*, 27(4), 471–86.

Clement, J. (1993) 'Using bridging analogies and anchoring intuitions to deal with students' preconceptions in physics', *Journal of Research in Science Teaching*, 30, 1241–57.

Coffield, F., Moseley, D., Hall, E. and Ecclestone, K. (2004) *Learning Styles and Pedagogy in Post-16 Learning: a systematic and critical review*, London: Learning and Skills Research Centre.

Coll, R.K. (2005) 'The role of models and analogies in science education', *International Journal of Science Education*, 27(2), 183–98.

Cuthbertson, A. and Frost, J. (2005) 'Public examinations', in J. Frost and T. Turner (eds), *Learning to Teach Science in the Secondary School: a companion to school experience*, 2nd edn, Abingdon: RoutledgeFalmer, 225–40.

Darby, L. (2005) 'Science students' perceptions of engaging pedagogy', *Research in Science Education*, 35(4), 425–45.

Daws, N. and Singh, B. (1999) 'Formative assessment strategies in secondary school science', *School Science Review*, 80(293), 71–8.

Deci, E.L., Vallerand, R.J., Pelletier, L.G. and Ryan, R.M. (1991) 'Motivation and education', *Educational Psychologist*, 26, 325–46.

DfES (Department for Education and Skills) (2004) *Pedagogy and Practice: teaching and learning in secondary schools*, London: DfES.

DfES (Department for Education and Skills) (2005) *Leading in Learning at Key Stage 3*, London: DfES.

Dobson, J. (2005) 'Assessing and monitoring progress in secondary science', in L.D. Newton (ed.), *Meeting the Standards in Secondary Science*, London: Routledge, 207–19.

ESRC (Economic & Social Science Research Council) (2005) ESRC 'Science in Society' workshop on diversity in science education and training, 1–2 February, workshop report.

Felder, R.M. (1988) 'Learning and teaching styles in engineering education', *Engineering Education*, 78(7) 674–81.

Feynman, R.P. (1998) *The Meaning of it All*, London: Penguin.

Frost, J. (2005) 'Planning for practical work', in J. Frost and T. Turner (eds), *Learning to Teach Science in the Secondary School: a companion to school experience*, 2nd edn, Abingdon: RoutledgeFalmer, 157–75.

Frost, J. and Turner, T. (eds) *Learning to Teach Science in the Secondary School: a companion to school experience*, 2nd edn, Abingdon: RoutledgeFalmer.

Gaither, C.C. and Cavazox-Gaither, A.E. (eds) (2002) *Chemically Speaking*, London: Institute of Physics, 191.

Gilbert, J. and Calvert, S. (2003) 'Challenging accepted wisdom: looking at the gender and science education question through a different lens', *International Journal of Science Education*, 25(7), 861–78.

Glynn, S.M. and Takahashi, T. (1998) 'Learning from analogy enhanced text', *Journal of Research in Science Teaching*, 35(10), 1129–49.

Hargreaves, L. and Galton, M. (2002) *Transfer from the Primary School: 20 years on*, London: RoutledgeFalmer.

Harrison, C. (2005) 'Assessing for learning', in J. Frost and T. Turner (eds), *Learning to Teach Science in the Secondary School: a companion to school experience*, 2nd edn, Abingdon: RoutledgeFalmer, 211–24.

Hayes, P. (1998) 'Assessment in the classroom', in M. Ratcliffe (ed.), *ASE Guide to Secondary Science*, Cheltenham: ASE/Stanley Thornes, 138–45.

Hein, T.L. (1999) 'Using writing to confront student misconceptions in physics', *European Journal of Physics*, 137–41.

Heywood, D. (2002) 'The place of analogies in science education', *Cambridge Journal of Education*, 32(2), 233–47.

Hollon, R.E., Roth, K.J. and Anderson, C.W. (1991) 'Science teachers' conceptions of teaching and learning', in J.E. Brophy (ed.), *Advances in Research on Teaching*, vol. 2, Greenwich: JAI Press, 145–86.

Honey, P. and Mumford, A. (1982) *Manual of Learning Styles*, London: P. Honey.

Hussain, (2005) 'What is science? Why Science Education?' in L.D. Newton (ed.), *Meeting the Standards in Secondary Science*, Abingdon: Routledge, 14–21.

Jackson, C. (2002) *Manual of the Learning Styles Profiler*. Available online: www.psi-press.co.uk.

Jenkins, E.W. (1999) 'School science, citizenship and the public understanding of science', *International Journal of Science Education*, 21(7), 703–10.

Jenkins, E.W. and Nelson, N.W. (2005) 'Important but not for me: students' attitudes towards secondary school science in England', *Research in Science and Technological Education*, 23(1), 41–57.

Jones, M. and Gott, R. 'Cognitive acceleration through science education: alternative perspectives', *International Journal of Science Education*, 20(7) 755–68.

Kennewell, S. (2004) *Meeting the Standards in using ICT for Secondary Teaching*, London: RoutledgeFalmer.

Keogh, B. and Naylor, S. (1999) 'Concept cartoons, teaching and learning in science: an evaluation', *International Journal of Science Education*, 21(4), 431–46.

Keogh, B. and Naylor, S. (2002) 'Dealing with differentiation', in S. Amos and R. Boohan (eds) *Aspects of Teaching Secondary Science*, London: RoutledgeFalmer.

Kolb, D. (1984) *Experiential Learning*, Englewood Cliffs: Prentice-Hall.

Kusukawa, S. and Maclean, I. (2006) *Transmitting Knowledge*, Oxford: Oxford University Press.

Lake, D. (2005) 'About being pure and natural', *International Journal of Science Education*, 27(4), 487–506.

Laugksch, R.C. (2000) 'Scientific literacy: a conceptual overview', *Science Education*, 84, 71–94.

Leinhardt, G., Putnam, R.T., Stein, M.K. and Baxter, J. (1991) 'Where subject knowledge matters', in J.E. Brophy (ed.), *Advances in Research on Teaching*, vol. 2, Greenwich: JAI Press, 87–114.

Levin, J.R., Morrison, C.R., McGivern, J.E., Mastropieri, M.A. and Scruggs, T.E. (1986) 'Mnemonic facilitation of text-embedded science facts', *American Educational Research Journal*, 23(4), 489–506.

Levinson, R. (2005a) 'Science for citizenship', in J. Frost and T. Turner (eds), *Learning to Teach Science in the Secondary School: a companion to school experience*, 2nd edn, Abingdon: RoutledgeFalmer, 251–69.

Levinson, R. (2005b) 'Beyond qualified teacher status: becoming a professional teacher', in J. Frost and T. Turner (eds), *Learning to Teach Science in the Secondary School: a companion to school experience*, 2nd edn, Abingdon: RoutledgeFalmer, 282–95.

McCarthy, B. (1980) *The 4MAT System*, Oakbrook: Excel Inc.

Maloney, J. (2005) 'Sex and health education', in J. Frost and T. Turner (eds), *Learning to Teach Science in the Secondary School: a companion to school experience*, 2nd edn, Abingdon: RoutledgeFalmer, 270–81.

Marzano, R.J. (1998) *A Theory-Based Meta-Analysis of Research on Instruction*,Colorado: Aurora.

Matthews, B. (2004) 'Promoting emotional literacy, equity and interest in science lessons for 11–14 year olds', *International Journal of Science Education*, 26(3), 281–308.

Miller, S. (2001) 'Public understanding of science at the crossroads', *Public Understanding of Science*, 10(1), 115–20.

Mind (2007) Available online: www.mind.org.uk.

Moallem, M. (1998) 'An expert teacher's thinking and teaching and instructional design model and principles', *Education, Training, Research and Development*, 46, 37–64.

Moseley, D., Baumfield, V., Elliott, J., Gregson, M., Higgins, S., Miller, J. and Newton, D.P. (2005) *Frameworks for Thinking*, Cambridge: Cambridge University Press.

Naylor, S., Keogh, B. and Goldsworthy, A. (2004) *Active Assessment*, London: Fulton.

Newton, D.P. (1988) *Making Science Education Relevant*, London: Kogan Page.

Newton, D.P. (1990) *Teaching with Text*, London: Kogan Page.

Newton, D.P. (1994) 'Supporting the comprehension of tabulated data', *British Educational Research Journal*, 20, 455–63.

Newton, D.P. (2000) *Teaching for Understanding*, London: Routledge-Falmer.

Newton, D.P. (2005) 'Motivating students in science', in L.D. Newton (ed.), *Meeting the Standards in Secondary Science*, London: Routledge.

Newton, D.P. and Merrell, C.H. (1994) 'Words that count: communicating with mathematical text', *International Journal of Mathematics in Science and Technology*, 25(3), 457–62.

Newton, D.P. and Newton, L.D. (1998) 'Primary children's conceptions of science and the scientist', *International Journal of Science Education*, 20(9), 1137–49.

Ofsted (Office for Standards in Education) (2003) *'Taking the first step forward towards an education for sustainable development'*, HMI 1658, London: Ofsted. Available online: www.ofsted.gov.uk.

Oniru, G.O.M. and Randell, E. (2006) 'Some aspects of students' understanding of a representational model of the particulate nature of matter in chemistry in three different countries', *Chemistry Education Research and Practice*, 7(4), 226–39.

Osborne, J. (2003) 'Attitudes towards science', *International Journal of Science Education*, 25(9), 1049–79.

Osborne, J. and Hennessy, S. (2006) *Report 6: Literature Review In Science Education and the Role of ICT*, Bristol: Futurelab Series. Available online: www.futurelab.org.uk/research/lit_reviews.htm.

Osborne, J., Simons, S. and Collins, S. (2003) 'Attitudes towards science: a review of the literature and its implications', *International Journal of Science Education*, 25(9), 1049–79.

Parker, L.H. and Rennie, L.J. (2002) 'Teachers' implementation of gender inclusive instructional strategies in single-sex and mixed-sex science classrooms', *International Journal of Science Education*, 24(9), 881–97.

Preece, P. and Baxter, J. (2000) 'Scepticism and gullibility: the superstitious and pseudo-scientific beliefs of secondary school students', *International Journal of Science Education*, 22(11), 1147–56.

QCA (Qualifications and Curriculum Authority) (2001) *Science: planning, teaching and assessing the curriculum for pupils with learning difficulties*, London: QCA.

QCA (Qualifications and Curriculum Authority) (2005) *Assessing Progress in Science*, London: QCA.

Reid, N. and Skryabina, E.A. (2003) 'Gender and physics', *International Journal of Science Education*, 25(4), 509–36.

Reiss, M. (2005) 'The nature of science', in J. Frost and T. Turner (eds), *Learning to Teach Science in the Secondary School: a companion to school experience*, 2nd edn, Abingdon: RoutledgeFalmer, 44–53.

Riding, R. and Raynor, S. (1999) *Cognitive Styles and Learning Strategies*, London: David Fulton.

Roberts, R. and Gott, R. (2004) 'Alternatives to coursework', *School Science Review*, 85(313), 103–8.

Rodrigues. S., Airnes, J. and Powell, M. (undated) *Ideas for Using Television Fiction in Science Classrooms*, and *Teachers Using Television Fiction in Science Classroom* (undated), Edinburgh University: The Institute for Science Education in Scotland.

Shamos, M. (1995) *The Myth of Scientific Literacy*, New Brunswick: Rutgers.

Singh, K., Granville, M. and Dika, S. (2002) 'Mathematics and science achievement: effects of motivation, interest, and academic achievement', *Journal of Educational Research*, 95(6), 323–32.

Sorenson, P. (2005) 'Teaching strategies and organising learning', in J. Frost and T. Turner (eds), *Learning to Teach Science in the Secondary School: a companion to school experience*, 2nd edn, Abingdon: RoutledgeFalmer.

Taber, K.S. (2001) 'When the analogy breaks down: modelling the atom on the solar system', *Physics Education*, 36(3), 222–6.

Thompson, M. (2006) *Supporting Gifted and Talented Pupils in the Secondary School*, London: Paul Chapman.

Transfer and Transition Project (2003) *Issue 2*, Cambridge University. Available online: creict.homerton.cam.ac.uk/transfer.

Tsai, C.-C. and Chou. C. (2002) 'Diagnosing students' alternative conceptions in science', *Journal of Computer Assisted Learning*, 18, 157–65.

Turner, T. (2005a) 'Beyond the classroom', in J. Frost and T. Turner (eds), *Learning to Teach Science in the Secondary School: a companion to school experience*, 2nd edn, Abingdon: RoutledgeFalmer.

Turner, T. (2005b) 'Reporting progress and accountability', in J. Frost and T. Turner (eds), *Learning to Teach Science in the Secondary School: a companion to school experience*, 2nd edn, Abingdon: RoutledgeFalmer, 241– 48.

Wallace, J. and Louden, W. (2003) 'What we don't understand about teaching for understanding: questions from science education', *Journal of Curriculum Studies*, 35(4), 545–66.

Weatherhead, H., Sandler, L. and Taylor, P. (2004) 'Falinge Park High School – raising the achievement of EAL learners in science', *School Science Review*, 86(314), 63–70.

Wellington, J. (1998) 'Dialogues in the science classroom', in M. Ratcliffe (ed.), *ASE Guide to Secondary Science*, Cheltenham: ASE/Stanley Thornes, 146–58.

Wellington, J. (2004) 'Multimedia in science teaching', in R. Barton (ed.), *Teaching Secondary Science with ICT*, Oxford: Oxford University Press.

Wellington, J. and Osborne, J. (2001) *Language and Literacy in Science Education*, Buckingham: Open University Press.

Wolpert, L. (1993) *The Unnatural Nature of Science*, Faber and Faber: London.

Wynn, C.M. and Wiggins, A.C. (1997) *The Five Biggest Ideas in Science*, New York: John Wiley.

Youens, B. (2005) 'Planning and evaluating lessons', in J. Frost and T. Turner (eds), *Learning to Teach Science in the Secondary School: a companion to school experience*, 2nd edn, Abingdon: RoutledgeFalmer, 125–40.

Zohar, A. (2006) 'Connected knowledge in science and mathematics education', *International Journal of Science Education*, 28(13), 1579–99.

WEBSITES

ASE	www.ase.org.uk
BECTA	www.becta.org.uk/
CLEAPSS	www.cleapss.org.uk
General Teaching Council for England	www.gtce.org.uk
Lifebytes	www.lifebytes.gov.uk/teachers
National Curriculum	www.nc.uk.net
National Curriculum in Action	www.ncaction.org.uk
Ofsted	www.ofsted.gov.uk
QCA	www.qca.org.uk
Routledge	www.routledge.com/textbooks/0415363926
TeacherNet	www.teachernet.gov.uk
Teacher Training Resource Bank	www.ttrb.ac.uk
UNESCO (ESD)	www.unesco.org/education/dsf

All websites accessed July 2007. Websites tend to be ephemeral. You should add or replace sites as needed.

Index